WILDFOWLING

An introduction
to shooting on the marsh
and foreshore

BASC Handbooks

WILDFOWLING

Edited by Jeffrey Olstead

Quiller

CONTRIBUTORS
Robin Marshall-Ball, Eric Begbie, Mark Cokayne,
Mark Greenhough, Jeffrey Olstead

PHOTOGRAPHS
Robin Marshall-Ball, Helen Baly, Mark Cokayne,
Rob Douglas, John Graham, Jeffrey Olstead, Nick Ridley,
Gaynor Roberts, Tom Wylie

DESIGNED BY
Sarah East and Sharyn Troughton

Copyright © 2008 BASC

First published in the UK in 2008
by Quiller, an imprint of Quiller Publishing Ltd

British Library Cataloguing-in-Publication Data
A catalogue record for this book
is available from the British Library

ISBN 978 1 84689 025 3

Printed in China

Quiller
An imprint of Quiller Publishing Ltd
Wykey House, Wykey, Shrewsbury, SY4 1JA
Tel: 01939 261616 Fax: 01939 261606
E-mail: info@quillerbooks.com
Website: www.countrybooksdirect.com

CONTENTS

1
WILDFOWLING ~ THE MAGIC AND THE MARSH

Take moonlight and frost, or the grey veils of morning dissolving into air and water, threaded by silver creeks, and all silent but for the crackle of ice or the soughing of the wind. Then hear, distantly, the yelp of geese, like hounds on a breast-high scent, swelling sharper and more urgently as the skeins close across the shining levels.

With every sense straining, nerves taut as a bowstring, the wildfowler knows an excitement that no other shooting sport can offer. Nor can it offer such disappointments. The wavering skeins pass two hundred feet overhead. The wigeon skim the tide a hundred yards away. Cold, wet and disconsolate, the wildfowler feels the magic evaporate; the mud, the marsh and the long walk home remain.

Wildfowling calls for hardiness, patience, a willingness to learn, and the ability to be content with a small bag – or none at all. And yet, of all shooting it is the most romantic, potentially the most dangerous and, many would say, represents the purest form of hunting. A wildfowler plies his or her trade in the remotest landscape and in the harshest conditions our winters can generate, in pursuit of the wildest of our fauna – many claim that it is the only truly wild sport left in these islands. Once Stanley Duncan memorably compared the wildfowler with the game shooter, saying 'He must be a better shot. He must endure hardships and dangers unknown in the other branch. He must be a trained ornithologist, learned in the habits and appearance of an infinite variety of birds.'

There is little doubt that wildfowling is the most challenging of shooting sports but, fortunately for those who would taste the wild magic of the marsh, it is also the most accessible.

Originally coastal wildfowling was undertaken for subsistence or to serve a very small local market, and in the nineteenth century those who ventured onto the marsh were often professional fowlers. The development of the puntgun and the advent of the railway made it possible for large quantities of duck, geese and wading birds to be shot in East Anglia and sent to Leadenhall Market in London.

However, from the early nineteenth century a handful of recreational shooters found their sport on the shore and during Victorian times punt gunning – shooting a single, large-bore gun from a canoe-shaped boat – became relatively popular.

At the beginning of the twentieth century there was a cadre of gentleman wildfowlers alongside an army of artisan fowlers who enjoyed

At the turn of the last century wildfowling was a sport for the gentleman and provided an income for the artisan

Wildfowlers at the Black Hut at Patrington Haven at the beginning of the twentieth century

almost unrestricted shooting. The solitary nature of wildfowling discouraged any clubs, and few felt the need for them. In that Edwardian twilight it would have been a far-sighted man indeed who perceived any threat to the future of the sport.

There was a far-sighted man. His name was Stanley Duncan. He was an engineer, living in Hull, whose passion was for wildfowling; he saw the threats presented by the destruction of coastal habitat and the increasingly raucous demands of the bird protectionists. According to tradition, which is perhaps romantic and may embroider the truth, he shared his fears with other wildfowlers who frequented a lonely, little, black-tarred hut at Patrington Haven on the banks of the Humber. There by the light of an oil lamp, an old stove stoked against the freezing blast, the germ of an idea was born.

What we know for certain is that, as a result of Duncan's initiative, the Wildfowlers' Association of Great Britain and Ireland (WAGBI) held its first general meeting at the Imperial Hotel, Hull, in April 1908. In 1981 WAGBI changed its name to the British Association for Shooting and Conservation, which today is the national representative body for wildfowling and all forms of live quarry shooting.

Just as the handful of fowlers who first met has evolved into a 127,000-strong organisation, so the world in which wildfowling takes place has changed beyond recognition. The first bird protection laws were introduced in 1880; they provided protection for most birds from the last day of February to the first day of August, but outside that period anything was fair game. So, until the Protection of Birds Act (1954), the wildfowler had an extraordinary range of quarry.

On 28 December 1908 one wildfowler shot eight mallard, three knot, one redshank and one dunlin, while his companions shot six larks, two

Wigeon over the Black Hut *by Julian Novorol, which hangs at the BASC head office at Marford Mill*

dabchicks, a woodpigeon and a kingfisher. Today, with a strictly limited quarry list, wildfowlers must have considerably greater skills as naturalists than their forebears. The old fowlers' saying, 'What's hit is history…what's missed is mystery', cannot now apply. With the wide variety of wading birds and other waterfowl that are protected, today's wildfowler must positively identify the approaching bird as a legitimate quarry species before even lifting the gun.

But, despite the restrictions, much of the magic still remains. When you cross the sea wall you enter a landscape that has largely escaped the heavy boot print of modern industry and agriculture. It is a remote and debatable land, governed by wind and tide, where raw Nature watches over the never-ending conflict between land and sea, far from the roar of motorway traffic and seldom afflicted by the light pollution of large conurbations. And, although the modern wildfowler is strictly limited in the species he or she may shoot, there is solace in the thought that one no longer needs to contend with muzzle-loading shotguns, oilskins and flannel underwear.

"It is a mark of a true sportsman to be contented with a small and hardly-earned bag of wild birds."

Sir Ralph Payne-Gallwey

Then and now

Just over a century ago Sir Ralph Payne-Gallwey offered some useful advice to the aspiring wildfowler on what to wear:

"Boots

Cowhide is admirable for these, as it is soft and pliable and dries quickly. India-rubber is at all times to be avoided, being unhealthy and unfit for use when fowling.

Outer clothes

Wear grey flannel trousers, waistcoat and coat, the former buttoning around the ankles on account of the long boots.

Sir Ralph P. Gallwey in fowling costume

A knitted fisherman's jersey with sleeves, made of wool, and worn over the waistcoat, is a wonderful preventative against cold.

Under clothes

Two tight-fitting flannel vests and drawers give more warmth (and are far easier to work in) than three sets of coats, waistcoats and trousers.

Food

A fowler should live well and treat himself generously, for we defy him to endure hard work and the severity of the elements on a poor diet."

2 WILDFOWLING IN THE TWENTY-FIRST CENTURY

Today's wildfowler shoots for the pot, not for profit. But don't expect to keep the deep-freeze full. Long hours on the marsh are seldom rewarded with a full bag. Nevertheless, however delicious a duck or goose may be when served at the dinner table, there are other rewards, more subtle and, in the twenty-first century, more precious than the weight of quarry.

Wildfowling is a solitary occupation. It will take you to remote and wild places, utterly removed from the rush and roar of the working world. Close to the pulse of nature you will see sights of extraordinary beauty, develop skills which tap deep into the hunting instinct and enjoy a richness of experience, tinged with danger, that is unequalled in any other sport. The danger is ever-present, but by planning and taking the proper precautions it can be minimised. What never diminishes is the wild beauty of the marsh. Not surprisingly this has tended to attract a particular kind of shooter and, as a result, has produced the richest of all shooting literature.

This is the place to start – read the great books and you will soon decide whether wildfowling is the sport for you. The lure of the marsh has changed little over the centuries, though the institutional framework certainly has. In England and Wales most wildfowling is controlled by local associations, and the first step for aspiring fowlers should be to contact a club in the area where they wish to shoot. BASC can give you advice on this and will also be able to tell you which clubs operate schemes for new members. It is clearly a huge benefit to be accompanied on your first wildfowling forays by an experienced member, but where that is not a strict requirement, the club secretary will almost certainly be able to put you in touch with a member who can act as mentor.

The second most important consideration, on the marsh, after safety, is quarry recognition. Under the Wildlife and Countryside Act 1981 all birds are protected. However, certain species may be shot during their open season. This means that in England and Wales the wildfowler can shoot nine species of duck, four species of geese, three waders, the moorhen and coot – though there are some differences in the rest of the UK. (*See Appendix II.*)

While it may be easy enough to recognise a wigeon or a pink-foot on an ornamental lake, it will be very different on the marsh. Poor light, foul weather and the need for snap decisions demand the highest standards of competence. Size, outline, flight pattern, sound and that indefinable quality that birdwatchers call 'jizz' need to be assessed rapidly and accurately. This is an aspect of wildfowling that is often underestimated, but instant recognition of quarry is a skill which itself can give great satisfaction.

Perhaps the greatest changes – certainly the greatest benefits – for wildfowlers in the twenty-first century come from the huge advances in weatherproof clothing. The testing conditions in which you will shoot mean that your clothing must be up to the job; the winter foreshore is a cold and exposed place where you will be crawling, and occasionally falling, in the mud. Rain, sleet and freezing winds are to be expected. Fortunately today's clothing can easily cope with this.

Remember that your gun also has to cope with these conditions. If you already shoot, your present gun will probably be more than adequate for wildfowling, but serious fowlers generally want to use something more suited to the sport. Apart from an understandable reluctance to expose an expensive gun to the ravages of salt and sand you may well want a gun that will handle magnum cartridges and is proofed for heavy loads of steel shot. We will look at this in greater detail in chapter 7.

Finally you will need a dog. It is not acceptable to shoot without the means of retrieving wounded birds – or dead ones that have fallen into an inaccessible spot. Again, this will be discussed in a later chapter but it is a serious consideration if you are thinking of taking up wildfowling.

QUARRY SPECIES

ENGLAND AND WALES

Tufted duck

Gadwall

Goldeneye

Mallard

Pintail

Pochard

Shoveler

Teal

Wigeon

Canada goose

Greylag goose

Pink-footed goose

White-fronted goose

Moorhen

Coot

Common snipe

Woodcock

Golden plover

SCOTLAND

White-fronted geese are protected. Otherwise the list is as for England and Wales.

NORTHERN IRELAND

As for England and Wales but with the addition of jack snipe curlew and scaup.

3 ACCESS TO THE FORESHORE

Historically the foreshore belongs to the Crown and for a long time there was assumed to be a right of free shooting. In essence this still exists in Scotland, however in the rest of the UK all foreshore shooting is controlled.

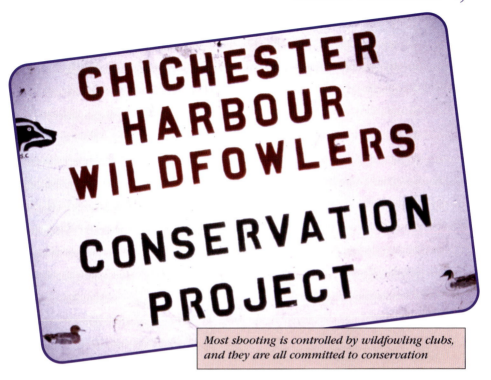

Most shooting is controlled by wildfowling clubs, and they are all committed to conservation

England, Wales and Northern Ireland

In the past the only real powers over the marsh were vested in county councils, which were able to make by-laws covering shooting. That is why wildfowling is still legal on a Sunday in some areas and not in others. When the 'free shooting' assumption was proved wrong, fowlers fell back on the defence that although you did not have a right to shoot on the foreshore, nobody had a right to stop you. That myth was exploded in a High Court judgement of 1967 that made any fowler liable to a charge of armed trespass.

WAGBI promptly took action to defend the sport and secured an agreement that its members would not be prosecuted for armed trespass when they shot over the Crown and Duchy of Lancaster foreshore. More recently, as greater regulation has been called for, the Crown requires clubs to hold proper shooting leases. The British Association for Shooting and Conservation (which succeeded WAGBI in 1981) negotiates on average fifteen new leases a year, securing the shooting over hundreds of miles of foreshore for its affiliated wildfowling clubs.

Those areas of the coastline that do not belong to the Crown can be controlled by a variety of interests. Over the years, parts of the Crown Estate foreshore have been sold off to various owners including local authorities, private individuals and the National Trust. In addition, local authorities control some areas under a regulating lease from the Crown Estate Commissioners and such a lease may, or may not, include the sporting rights.

The programme of securing land for shooting on the Crown foreshore has now ended. All known available areas that might interest wildfowlers have been looked at by the Joint Group for Wildfowling and Conservation over Tidal Land (JTG). This group, which is a partnership between BASC, the Crown Estate, Natural England, the Countryside Council for Wales and the Environment and Heritage Service Northern Ireland, has set a timetable to bring these areas under lease agreements.

It was fortunate that wildfowling clubs existed all around our coast and were in a position to take on leases, which prevented the shooting falling into the hands of individuals, or those who would ban the sport.

Scotland

In Scotland, the right to recreation on the foreshore is a right held by the Crown for all to enjoy. Shooting is deemed to be a recreational activity and therefore wildfowling is widely available. Foreshore in Scotland is defined as 'that area of ground between the mean high and low water marks of ordinary spring tides'. However, this right has been modified in certain areas such as harbours, Ministry of Defence ground, etc. Several local and national reserves (LNRs and NNRs) have been declared over Scottish foreshore, and on some of these sites wildfowling is allowed through a permit system.

The Land Reform (Scotland) Act (2003) and accompanying Scottish Outdoor Access Code introduced a number of changes with respect to shooting, including wildfowling, from February 2005. In the past wildfowlers had to ensure that they accessed foreshore legally, along a public right of way for example. The new Access Code (Section 2.12) allows those carrying shotguns to cross land responsibly for immediate access to areas of land or water where they have the right to shoot, and then return. This avoids the requirement to use public rights of way. Visiting wildfowlers who are not sure of the regulations should contact BASC Scotland.

The morning's bag

4 GETTING STARTED

Because wildfowling is a solitary sport wildfowlers are, perhaps, not naturally the most clubbable people. Indeed clubs have, in most cases, only recently appeared on the wildfowling scene.

Until the 1950s little had changed in the sport for a century. The old closed season, which ran from the end of February to August 1, was lengthened but otherwise the threat, perceived by Stanley Duncan so long before, lay dormant. It erupted after the Second World War, culminating in the Protection of Birds Act (1954), when WAGBI fought a vigorous and largely successful campaign to defend wildfowling. This battle galvanised wildfowlers and all over the country they began to form clubs to protect their interests. In 1950 WAGBI had five affiliated clubs; by 1960 there were over two hundred. Today, wherever on the coast you want to shoot, there will probably be a local wildfowling club. And, despite increasing restrictions, the sport continues to thrive.

You should find an experienced guide for your first visits to the marsh

In general the clubs manage their shooting in accordance with club rules, agreed management plans and the BASC wildfowling code of practice. A surprisingly large area is protected and many clubs provide their own wildfowl refuges. Out of the total of 105,000 hectares that clubs control more than 90 per cent is scheduled as Sites of Special Scientific Interest or is designated under conservation law. (In comparison, all the RSPB reserves amount to 130,000 hectares.) It is a tribute to the sustainability of properly managed wildfowling that it is permitted in so many sensitive areas, but fowlers must always be aware of the responsibility they bear. One careless or cavalier act could endanger everybody's sport.

Clubs vary enormously. At one end of the scale you will find a small association that controls a single marsh or estuary, is run on a shoestring and provides little more than access to the foreshore. Typically its annual subscription will cost only a few pounds more than BASC membership, which is fully included. So in reality your fowling may be costing you less than £10 a year. At the other end of the scale are large clubs that own or control a significant area of foreshore and may well offer other shooting opportunities inland. They may have a good social programme, run conservation initiatives and, most importantly, provide help and instruction for newcomers, often including a guided introduction to the marsh. These benefits will, necessarily, be reflected in their subscription rates.

Most clubs will require, at the least, an interview with the committee before you are accepted as a member. The larger clubs will often require you to pass a test, typically covering quarry recognition, the law, safety, club rules and wildfowling practice. This may be coupled with a probationary period during which some, or all, of your visits to the marsh must be accompanied by a club member. For most people that is a very positive benefit. The marsh is a daunting place and to be able to share the experience of an old hand is invaluable.

If the club does not insist upon it you would still be wise to seek out a member who is willing to accompany you on your first few visits. This will make a huge difference to the sport you enjoy, and to your peace of mind. Even the experienced fowler is handicapped if he or she visits a new venue without the benefit of local knowledge; acquiring it should be your first objective.

BASC has full details of just under two hundred affiliated clubs and will be able to advise you on which ones in your chosen area have vacancies and what they offer. Members of BASC can also take advantage of the wildfowling permit scheme. This is a unique facility that allows any member to obtain day-tickets from forty wildfowling clubs scattered throughout the UK. There are various conditions and sometimes it is a requirement that you are accompanied by a member. This, again, is a great benefit. If you are considering taking up wildfowling and would like to try the sport before applying to join a club the permit scheme offers an ideal introduction.

Apart from the provisions made by clubs for new members, there are no formal training schemes for wildfowling. However, you might consider going out with a professional guide. In Scotland BASC has a register of approved goose guides and the association's Scottish centre will be happy to give advice. A number of guides also operate in other parts of the UK and advertise in the shooting press.

Before going out it is sensible to get a good theoretical knowledge of the sport, and there are many books on wildfowling that are worth reading. While this is no substitute for first-hand experience it will prepare you for the adventure and help you to interpret the experience and gain more from it. You may also be less of an embarrassment to your guide.

BASC Members'
Wildfowling Permits
2007/2008

Participating clubs, fieldcraft, safety and the law

BASC

5 GETTING THE GEAR

So, you've read the books and articles about wildfowling. Tucked up in the armchair you've heard the clamour of grey geese under a winter moon, the soft whistle of wigeon skimming the frost-rimed reeds, you've toppled moon-raking mallard, pummelled by the storm, your eyes stinging from the salt spray, and now you're bursting to try the real thing.

Fair enough. There is a magic, but unless your personal magic extends to walking on the water, you must go into this sport with your eyes open. On the marsh and the foreshore you will encounter the harshest and wildest of conditions, so before you rush off to find a club, or contact the BASC permit scheme, make sure you have the right kit for the job. The environment is harsh; perfect wildfowling weather is a fierce gale driving horizontal rain, or the shimmer of frost forming on your gun barrels as dawn starts to break.

Your feet are probably the first thing to consider. Waders are the norm for fowlers, with a choice of materials and lengths. Many prefer thigh waders, with a cut off pair of waterproof trousers covering their bottom; others prefer chest waders, as they cover all the areas that may get wet or muddy. If you have a long walk to your chosen shooting spot, chest waders can become uncomfortably warm. On the other hand, slipping into a gutter can easily fill a thigh wader with freezing water, and that can be uncomfortably cold. As a compromise you can try waist waders, which allow you to sit down in the wet but do not restrict, or protect, your upper body. Marshes vary in their character and, as usual, if you are not sure about the most suitable gear, seek local advice.

Waders are generally designed for fishermen, so remember that their requirements may be different. Felt soles are fine on a rocky stream but only an experienced off-piste skier would try them on mud. Rubber cleated soles are the best – and usually the cheapest – and studs can be a big help. Stocking-foot waders are increasingly popular and these are worth considering, especially because the separate wading boots will provide greater ankle support and are usually more comfortable, and more durable, if you have long distances to walk.

You also have a choice of wader materials. Neoprene is warm and flexible and makes great waders; again, though, think of the distance you may have to walk. This also applies to PVC waders, which are cheap and practical but, as they do not 'breathe', can easily turn into a mobile sauna. To overcome this problem various types of breathable waders are now available. These are light and comfortable but can be pricey, less flexible than neoprene – which is an important consideration when trying to swing a gun while huddled in the mud – and they are also more easily damaged.

If you do opt for chest waders, one point worth looking at is the position of the shoulder strap buckles – on some examples the buckle is located exactly where you will mount the gun's stock on your shoulder. Firing a heavy-recoiling cartridge could leave a very pretty buckle-shaped bruise on your shoulder, not to mention a broken buckle!

One final piece of advice on boot-foot waders: try to get ones that are reasonably tight around the ankles. This not only saves on socks and blisters, but the last thing you want is to leave your waders behind in the mud. Old hands frequently recommend tying a strap or cord round the instep and the ankle of the waders to prevent these problems, but there is another school of thought which argues that, in an extreme situation, with your foot trapped in mud, slipping out of your wader is the only alternative to becoming trapped, and a strap would prevent this.

What you wear inside the boots warrants a little consideration. Most people swear by woollen socks since they will keep you warm even when they are wet. The ones with a loopstitch foot provide extra warmth, and help to stop the water sloshing around if you do get wet. There are also various bootees on the market that can make a big difference to your comfort and insoles are an absolute must. Silk may not contribute to the rugged image of the wildfowler, but silk under-socks are legendary heat retainers and may add much to his comfort. (The same can be said for silk underwear.) Remember, though, that too much insulation can be as bad as too little if it makes the boots so tight that they inhibit the insulating quality of whatever you are wearing under them.

Coats are also of paramount importance for fowling, and you are always looking for a compromise. You want something to keep you warm on an arctic morning, waterproof to keep out the driving rain, yet light enough to avoid overheating when walking out onto the marsh. Add to this the need for appropriate camouflage, and you start to see how difficult it can be to select a suitable coat, especially when confronted by the bewildering selection available at most gun shops and country outfitters.

Ramblers, struggling to the summit of a modest bump in the Cotswolds but kitted out for the north face of the Eiger, often suffer the countryman's derision, but we can learn a thing or two from them. In particular, the benefits of a layered system can prevent some of the problems associated with a long tramp across the mud, carrying a sackful of decoys, followed by even longer inactivity, crouched in the freezing mud and rain.

So let's begin with the fundamentals: the undergarments. Thermals are incredibly useful, and come in many varieties. Some manufacturers produce thermals especially for sportsmen – and women, – which are designed to cope with strenuous activity. Just remember that a walk may be involved, so you don't want anything that chafes, retains moisture or is too hot. You only end up sweating like a pig on the way out, then sitting for three hours in freezing weather and damp thermals.

After a synthetic layer next to the skin, which wicks away sweat, a fleece that continues that process is an obvious choice. You may opt for one or two layers of fleece or a quilted waistcoat. To top it there are some good windproof fleeces available now which – unless it is actually raining, or worse – may keep you at a comfortable temperature while you are active. The coat can then be donned to keep you warm while you wait.

Every wildfowler has his, or her, idea of the perfect coat and no two would agree, but there are certain essentials. Starting at the top, a hood is an absolute necessity. Because two-thirds of your body heat is lost through the head and neck make sure it offers as little opportunity as possible for wind and rain to penetrate, and, most importantly, it should tighten round

The army surplus greatcoat tied up with string is no longer de rigueur for wildfowlers. Now there is a specialist jacket to suit every pocket and need

your face with enough freedom for you to turn your head without becoming blindfolded. A peak is crucial for keeping the rain out of your eyes, so if the hood doesn't have one make sure there's room for a cap underneath, and it's not a bad idea to make sure that you can get a balaclava under your cap.

On the marsh you cannot adopt the comfortable, balanced stance of the game shooter. You're probably crouching in a gutter with the birds arriving from every direction except the expected one. Freedom of movement is therefore of paramount importance in any coat – especially if you are also wearing several pullovers, fleeces, quilties and mum's old fur coat.

Provided the sleeves are loose enough, you should now consider the cuffs. Sitting clutching your gun it is almost inevitable that your arms will be pointing skywards and the cuffs will become little buckets to collect the rain. Look for a neoprene lining that will act like a wetsuit and keep you relatively snug. It goes without saying that the coat must be impervious to the elements and should let perspiration out while keeping the heat in. Most other considerations are matters of personal preference, though the length of the coat should be related to your waders. To stay dry it needs to cover the tops of thigh waders, but that could limit freedom of movement – especially if you are sitting on the tail of it. For chest waders a shorter jacket can have advantages, especially where deep wading may be involved.

In fact most fowlers have a selection of coats for different uses and different times of year and weather conditions. The extreme traditionalist may even be spotted in an old army greatcoat, but it must be admitted that modern high-tech coats with breathable waterproof membranes are an absolute godsend for the fowler.

It is also important to remember a hat and gloves. Again these may be high-tech materials or simple woolly ones, depending on personal preference, but while wool retains its insulating properties when wet, it may not be so comfortable. On certain parts of our coast it seems that a black woolly bobble hat is the in thing to wear – strange choice as it does nothing for concealment. Scan any marsh as the light strengthens after a dawn flight and you will easily pick out the black-bobble fowlers – and if you can see them you can be doubly sure the wildfowl can. Whatever your choice of headgear, make sure it is in a subdued colour that merges with the environment.

Anyone who can keep their hands dry on the marsh is probably not carrying a gun, and if you are wearing polar mittens you are probably not firing one; here again technology comes to the rescue. There is a good selection of gloves on the market specifically designed for shooting. Some fowlers opt for wearing thin leather gloves under woollen fold-back mittens – this keeps the hands warm in bitter weather and, with the mitten of the trigger hand folded back, allows for easier use of the triggers when the need arises.

6 STAYING ALIVE

So, at this point our heads, hands and bodies are warm and dry. We want to stay like that, which is why we now move onto the less glamorous issues such as staying alive. This is the basic survival kit.

NEVER forget your tide table, and learn to understand what it means. You may be the best camouflaged, best kitted-out fowler on the marsh, but when they cut off your silk long johns in the mortuary, it doesn't much matter. The sea can, and does, kill. If you don't understand it, it will beat you. If you're not sure what all the information in your tide table means, ask. Try to understand what a huge effect the weather can have on the tide. A proper understanding can not only ensure that you avoid danger, it can also allow you to shoot in the prime spot for longer because you know what is happening with the tide. These points will be fully explained in chapter 8 but for now it is enough to remember this: never venture onto the marsh without your tide table.

Another key aid to staying dry is a wading staff. This is simply a long sturdy stick. Use it for probing any water, especially in the dark. It will tell you how deep the water is and also whether the bottom is deep, claggy mud or firm sand. It is also good practice to probe the ground as you walk out, because little creeks, often referred to as ankle breakers, can be detected using the staff before you put your foot into them.

Most scare stories about wildfowling involve fog, and there is good reason for this. The marsh can be a barren, featureless place with few landmarks at the best of times. Drop a pea-souper on top of this and you have a recipe for disaster. Always carry a compass, and know how to use it. You should at least know north and south on the marsh, and also know how to walk to a bearing. An obvious point but still worth mentioning: don't hold the compass anywhere near your gun when taking a reading as the proximity of the metal may give a false reading and send you off in the wrong direction.

Modern fowlers can also use a global positioning system (GPS). Originally developed for the military, these hand held boxes provide a number of very useful features. Firstly, they work as a compass. Secondly, they tell you exactly where you are, and will also give you information such as distance travelled and speed. Probably most useful, however, is the ability to enter waypoints. A waypoint is just a register of a point, entered either by pressing a button when you are there, or by grid reference. It is also possible to link a series of waypoints to form a route. This will provide a simple guide to getting off the marsh in bad conditions, but, often more usefully, a simple guide to finding those hot spots occasionally encountered where flightline and cover for the fowler converge.

Torch - Should be waterproof, as bright as possible for its size, and always check the batteries before going out.

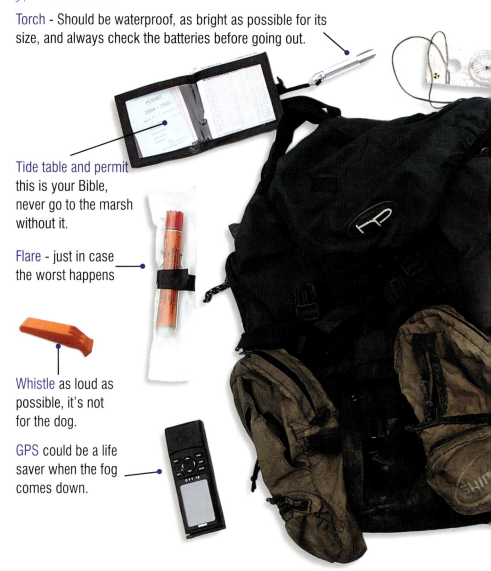

Tide table and permit this is your Bible, never go to the marsh without it.

Flare - just in case the worst happens

Whistle as loud as possible, it's not for the dog.

GPS could be a life saver when the fog comes down.

It is also essential to carry a torch and a whistle. Waterproof torches with halogen bulbs can be seen at a great distance, but check the batteries before each outing. If the worst happens, and you get stuck on the marsh, a light and whistle could make all the difference to rescuers reaching you before the tide does. It is also common practice now for fowlers to carry their mobile phones, again just in case the worst happens. If you are fowling with a friend you may also consider taking short range VHF radios.

Compass know the lie of the marsh, and the safe direction to get off it

Food and warm drink to keep you alert

Two way radio useful if you're fowling with a friend. Make sure you have spare batteries

Mobile phone Always make sure your battery is fully charged

The essential kit to take onto the foreshore

READY TO GO?

Use this check list to make sure you are prepared for the marsh

ESSENTIAL FOR SAFETY

Compass
Whistle
Wading staff
Tide table
Torch
Mobile phone

USEFUL FOR SAFETY

Two-way radio
Flare
Flask of tea/coffee
Sandwiches or emergency food

These are easily obtained and are useful for communicating, especially if you have and accident.

Always make sure you have a hot drink and some food with you, it is amazing how much better you feel after a hot coffee in the cold weather. Remember that fowlers have been known to suffer from hypothermia. Finally, always tell someone where you are going, and when you expect to get back from the marsh.

7 GUNS FOR THE MARSH

There was a time when any sporting gun was called a 'fowling piece', and it's still true that almost any 12 bore gun will do for wildfowling. If you are already a game or clay shot your existing shotgun will probably suffice. But…

While, for occasional forays onto the foreshore, a 12 bore game gun is perfectly adequate, within its limitations of range, if you are serious about wildfowling you will need the proper tool for the job.

The first consideration is the nature of the marsh itself. Its chief components are mud, sand and water – salt water. This is what your gun will be exposed to every time you cross the sea wall. Clearly it must be rugged and reliable; you will fall over, submerge it, get grit in the action and submit it to the kind of abuse which no well-bred game gun would appreciate. Ease of cleaning, both inside and out, is important. It follows from this that you will not be looking at the top end of the price range – many a top quality game gun has been ruined by exposure to quite normal wildfowling conditions. Because appearance is less important than performance, many people will opt for a second-hand gun, but do make sure it has been thoroughly checked by a gunsmith. After walking miles across the mud, freezing for an hour and then getting the only shot of the flight, the last thing you want to hear is the feeble click of a misfire.

While fowlers are noted, one might say notorious, for using large bore guns, the beginner is more likely to opt for a conventional 12 bore shotgun. Using other gauges can have advantages, though these are hotly debated, and the time may come when you long to heft a mighty 4 bore to your shoulder, swing like the for'ard battery of HMS *Renown* and disappear in a cloud of smoke and thunder when you pull the trigger. That time is not likely to be yet.

Choosing a wildfowling gun

Although a conventional game gun is fine for the occasional foray onto the marsh the regular wildfowler will probably need a rather more specialised firearm – with the environment's corrosive and erosive combination of salt water and mud, it is not the place to wield your grandfather's beloved Purdey, or any other valuable gun for that matter.

The ideal weapon is robust, reliable, uncomplicated and inexpensive. When we crest the sea wall we leave the twenty-first century behind and enter a timeless world governed by wind and tide, a land of saltings, spartina grass, and deep muddy creeks. This mud is special. Unlike the mud of a freshly ploughed inland field, coastal mud is fine grained, gritty, soft, and very mobile.

Types of shotgun

Pump-action

Semi-automatic (three-shot)

Over-and-under

Side-by-side

The surface of the mud is lifted by the waters of a rising tide (have you ever seen clear water in an estuary?) and deposited as a thin coating on any marsh vegetation that the tide covers. When the tide ebbs the wind dries off the plants and the mud particles are blown off in what is in effect a 'diluted' sandstorm. No matter how careful you are, your gun will get muddy as a matter of course. This happens by direct contact with the ground surface, by being handled by mud-smeared hand or glove, and even by the ingress of wind-blown particles, yet it will still be required to function perfectly when the chance of a shot comes.

In choosing your fowling piece, you have a choice of two types of double-barrelled gun, single-barrelled self-loading and pump-action guns, bolt-action repeaters and even single-shot weapons. When faced with this bewildering choice of shotgun types that are all marketed for wildfowling, you need to consider very carefully the merits and disadvantages of each design.

Shotgun type	Advantages	Disadvantages	Comments
Single-shot shotguns	• Usually simple and robust mechanism • Very inexpensive • Easy to maintain • Operates when muddy externally	• Limits the shooter to single shots • Usually lightweight – gives punishing recoil with heavy loads • Single choice of choke/cartridge	Useful as a 'knockabout' gun but its limiting factors outweigh its advantages
Pump-action	• Three-shot capability • Usually heavy enough to handle heavy loads • Simple and robust mechanism	• Slide mechanism and loading port easily clogs up with mud so reloading fails • Breech susceptible to ingress of mud – this jams the action • Single choice of choke/cartridge • Difficult to check for barrel obstructions	Fine for inland wildfowl shooting

Shotgun type	Advantages	Disadvantages	Comments
Self (auto)-loader	• Three-shot capability • Gas operation reduces recoil • Some available with $3^{1}/_{2}$" chambers for larger loads	• Breech and loading port susceptible to ingress of mud that jams the action • May fail to reload less powerful cartridges • Single choice of choke/cartridge • Difficult to check for barrel obstructions	Fine for inland wildfowl shooting; popular on the marsh but needs more care and the most reliable models tend to be expensive
Over-and-under double	• Instant choice of choke/cartridge • Simple and robust mechanism • Easy reloading • Some available with $3^{1}/_{2}$" chambers for larger loads	• Ejector/extractor mechanisms susceptible to mud-clogging • Wide gape when opened – difficult in cramped hide	The versatility of two barrels makes this a good choice for the coast, but make sure the ejector mechanisms are kept clean
Side-by-side double	• Instant choice of choke/cartridge • Simple and robust mechanism • Easy reloading • The most 'mud-proof' of all shotguns • Inexpensive	• Ejector/extractor mechanisms susceptible to mud-clogging	Though less fashionable, this is a gun for the foreshore, especially in its boxlock non-ejector form

From the above table you will see that a bog-standard, double-barrelled, side-by-side, or over-and-under, emerges as a good choice for the foreshore. It has the fewest exposed moving parts, and it field strips into three simple pieces so that any mud or grit can be quickly wiped away from the breech and barrel flats. With drop-open guns the bores can be checked quickly for mud, snow, or any other obstructions – a critically important safety factor in such a demanding environment – and changing from duck to goose cartridges when a skein appears over the sea wall is easy, silent, and quick. Over all these guns can provide distinct advantages with a modest price.

However, it must be said that among today's wildfowlers, semi-automatics are probably the most widely used guns. They give you an extra shot, are particularly good at reducing the recoil from heavy cartridges, and probably more shore gunners swear by their autos than swear at them. They are becoming increasingly reliable, but that reliability comes at a price and the best guns do not fall into the budget category.

You have to accept that a fowling piece is by its very nature a knockabout gun that will be exposed to conditions well beyond the demands of any form of inland shooting, so do not break the bank to acquire a fine example of gunmaking artistry if you intend to go down to the sea. In the final analysis, after considering all the pros and cons in the table above, you must choose the style of gun with which you feel most comfortable.

Chosing the right bore

 ### 12 Bore

The overwhelming majority of wildfowlers use a 12 bore and there are good reasons for this choice:
- It will deal with almost every situation you are likely to meet
- It is easy to shoot
- It is easy to carry
- It handles a wide range of ready-loaded cartridges at affordable prices
- With longer chambers available - up to 31/2" - it can cope with most quarry species
- It can be used for game or rough shooting and clays

Although you may have to carry the gun some distance it will usually be slung over your shoulder in a gun-slip so weight is not as crucial as it might be for other disciplines. However, in the half light you may have to swing onto duck very quickly, and you will probably be in a cramped position with many additional layers of clothing, so bear in mind that extra pounds and extra inches may not improve your performance. Longer barrels certainly do not give you a longer reach.

Weight does enter the equation because you may want a gun that is proofed for heavy or high-performance loads - especially steel - so it needs to be heavy enough to handle these loads safely and absorb the recoil.

A wildfowling gun will therefore weigh between 7½ and 8 lbs (roughly 3.5 kg) and have a minimum of 3" (76 mm) chambers, although recently some shooters have been opting for 3½" (89 mm) for reasons that will be explained when we consider cartridges.

Proofing has become complicated, and the criteria change from time to time. As a result you should always ensure, by talking to your dealer or a gunsmith, that the gun you are buying is suited to the shooting you want to do and will safely handle the loads you intend to use.

 ## 10 Bore

Some of the major manufacturers produce 10 bore guns for wildfowling. The argument for using a bigger bore gun is that it will handle the heavy loads of some non-lead shot much better than a stretched 12 bore. It is also claimed that the increased diameter of the cartridge case means that fewer pellets are deformed in contact with the barrel when the gun is fired, and therefore shot patterns and penetration are better.

There are, of course, disadvantages. A limited range of ready-loaded cartridges is available and they are expensive – at least twice the cost of similar loads for a 12 bore. Many fowlers using this gauge load their own but that is not recommended for the absolute beginner.

Other disadvantages include increased weight, and the design of some modern 10 bores. A 10 bore chambered for 3½" (89 mm) cartridges should weigh between 9 and 10 lb to absorb the recoil of hurling 2 or more ounces (57 g) of non-lead into the winter dawn – that is far heavier than even a magnum 12. This additional weight may be an important factor, as you often have to walk a long way carrying it. And these are not light and handy weapons that you can casually throw to your shoulder as a party of teal flashes over your head in the pre-dawn murk!

As well as the conventional double-barrelled guns, a number of semi-automatic or self-loading 10 bores are available. While these are powerful weapons, they require much more care and attention to prevent them becoming mud-clogged out on the saltmarsh.

Finally, a 10 bore, like its bigger brothers, is a dedicated and specialist wildfowling calibre – you will not use it on a game shoot or from a pigeon hide.

For the vast majority of wildfowling situations, the magnum 12 must be considered to be the ideal starter weapon. Only when the bug really bites, and your imagination becomes clouded with the vision of vast skeins of geese in the wildest of our coastal environments, will you begin to hanker after something bigger, heavier, and more cumbersome than your 12 bore. The 10 bore is the smallest of the wildfowler's heavy artillery.

 ## Big bores - the mighty 8 and 4 bores

There are those who believe that nothing but an 8 or 4 bore is good enough and they will delight in telling you so – often at considerable length. There may indeed be some benefits, and these guns may be great fun to shoot with, but…

These are guns for the dedicated goose shooter. In the days of lead shot, the 8 and 4 bores gave the shooter a distinct increase in effective range over the magnum 12, producing killing patterns at 65 yards with 8 bores and 75 yards with the mighty 4. Nowadays their chief advantage is in providing a sufficiently dense pattern of non-lead shot in sizes large enough to penetrate and kill wild geese at ranges out to perhaps 50 yards for the 8 and 60 yards with a 4.

It must be remembered, however, that the longer the range the more skilled the shooter must be. This means that he or she must be capable of consistently hitting the target in the middle of the pattern at these ranges. This will only come with much foreshore experience with lesser guns. Even then only a few fowlers can achieve it consistently.

A very limited number of 8 bore cartridges is still produced commercially, but ammunition for both 8 and 4 bores really belongs to the realm of the home loader. Let's just say they are probably not ideal for beginners.

Choke

Choke is a narrowing of the inside of the muzzle end of the gun barrel. Traditionally it has been believed that the 'tighter' the choke – in other words, the greater the amount of constriction relative to the true cylinder – the denser the pattern of pellets leaving the gun should be. We generally talk about 'degrees of choke' and they are nowadays usually described, starting with the tightest, as full choke, three-quarters, half, and a quarter. A double-barrelled gun will usually have a tighter choke in its second barrel, on the assumption that the bird will be farther away when you fire the second barrel. Some over-and-unders, and most single-barrel guns, take screw-in chokes, which give you the ability to select whichever you think is most appropriate.

As soon as the cloud of shot leaves the muzzle it starts to spread out. There comes a point where the individual pellets are so widely dispersed

The image (top right), exaggerated for clarity, shows how the barrel can be bored for choke. A tighter constriction will generally produce a tighter pattern of shot. The middle picture shows the least degree of choke - improved cylinder - while the bottom picture shows full choke, which is the tightest. Note that a tighter choke does not always extend the range of a cartridge; it merely increases the density of pattern in most shots.

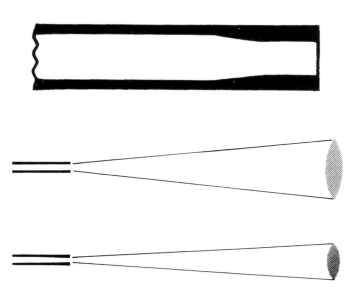

that too few will strike the vital organs of the quarry to guarantee a clean kill. The theory of choke is that producing a denser cloud of shot at the muzzle will hold the pattern together for longer. Theoretically, then, at a longer range the pellets are still in a dense enough formation to kill.

So, the conventional wisdom is that a tight choke will give the ability to take shots at longer range, and that, for a wildfowler, is very desirable.

However, recent research by BASC has cast some doubt on the validity of this assumption. The results are complex and need careful interpretation. What they do reveal is an extraordinary degree of variability. In practice this means that while a tighter choke may, on average, produce a more killing pattern at slightly longer range, it will not necessarily do so with every cartridge. Even from the same box, one cartridge may hold its pattern at a certain distance while another breaks down.

Because shots do tend to be taken at longer ranges on the foreshore than inland, wildfowlers prefer a more tightly choked gun, and that is a sensible choice. However, you should never assume that tighter chokes will extend your range. There is no substitute for accuracy – that is putting your pattern on a target at a range where enough pellets will penetrate the vital organs. And remember that while some Shots can do that consistently at 40 yards, the average Shot, which may well include you, can only do it at 30 yards or less.

Comparative wildfowling cartridges

4 bore   *8 bore*   *10 bore*   *12 bore*

Cartridges

Shot sizes

Shot sizes that are in general use range from No. 9 (the smallest) to AAA (the largest). Unfortunately different countries use different numbering systems, so American shot is roughly one size larger than the UK equivalent number. This may not be clear on the box.

There is a further complication: although all shot of a given size, say UK No. 3, should have the same diameter it may have different weights. For instance, steel No. 3 shot (tungsten-based) weighs, very roughly, 30 per cent less than lead pellets, while Hevi-shot weighs 10 per cent more.

In practice this means that for lead alternatives, apart from Hevi-shot and similar dense shot types, you should increase the size from the loads that were traditionally recommended. Some of the old books are very specific in their recommendations – No. 6 for teal, No. 4 for mallard and so on. Unfortunately, sitting on the marsh, you can never predict which particular species is going to appear at a particular moment. The best rule, therefore, is to err on the side of caution. Better a heavily shot teal than a lightly pricked, and lost, mallard.

Recent studies in America, and by BASC in the UK, indicate that we should be using larger pellets than of old. These have more energy to penetrate vital organs. However the size, or weight, of the pellet is only part of the equation and your choice of cartridge will be determined by a number of factors.

Performance

In Great Britain (but not yet Northern Ireland) it is illegal to use lead on the foreshore. New types of shot are being developed but for now we can only consider the main options that are currently available: bismuth, tungsten matrix, Hevi-shot and steel.

Before looking at the individual properties of these substances it is important to understand what the cartridge is expected to do. Put very simply, it has to deliver enough pellets each with enough energy to ensure a clean kill. That happens when sufficient pellets hit vital organs (e.g brain or heart). A small bird with smaller organs, contained within a smaller area, requires a denser cloud of shot than a larger bird and, because they have to penetrate less muscle, the pellets can be smaller.

Wildfowl are generally large birds. A Canada goose can weigh up to 6½ kg (14 lb), while the commonest duck, the mallard, will weigh about 1 kg (2+ lb) – they represent large but well-padded targets. This means that, while fewer pellets are needed to ensure hitting its vital organs, those pellets must still have the energy to penetrate the feathers, skin and muscle before hitting the organs. A larger pellet, being heavier, will carry a greater punch and, as a result, you will use larger shot sizes than most game or pest shooters. The most appropriate size will be determined by the size of the quarry, the type of shot you are using, and the range at which you can consistently hit your target.

However, upon entering the gun shop you will be faced with a bewildering array of 12 bore cartridges, not only of different sizes but of different weights. First consider the length of the cartridge. Many older English game guns are restricted to 2½" (65 mm) but for a standard modern game gun it is 2¾" (70 mm), and those are the longest cartridges you can use. A magnum 12 bore will usually have a 3" (76 mm) chamber which means that you can fire cartridges up to that length, and some are now produced with a 3½" (89 mm) chamber, which allows even longer cartridges. It will fire shorter ones, but then you lose the advantage of a magnum. That advantage is obvious: a longer cartridge can hold more pellets, so it should throw a denser pattern.

But life is never simple, and within the different cartridge lengths you will find a variety of loads available. For instance, a standard 2¾" game gun can handle loads from 1 oz (28 g) to 1¼ oz (36 g) provided it is proved to that level.

So, if you're wildfowling, why not go for the big loads? Well, by all means try them – preferably starting by patterning your gun at a shooting ground (see page 51). You may find that the pattern is distorted, the recoil causes an involuntary flinch, or any one of many reasons why your shooting may become less accurate or effective. Ultimately it comes down to personal experience. What we need to find is the most effective combination – something that delivers the right number of pellets of the right size. It is up to you, the wildfowler, to put them in the right place.

The advantage of a magnum is that it can handle the heavier loads without stress, on the gun or on the shooter. The denser load means that more pellets should hit the bird, increasing the likelihood of striking vital organs and so ensuring an instant kill. As an indication of the increased number of pellets a magnum load gives you here are the approximate pellet counts for 12 bore number 3 (lead) shot:

Length	Weight of shot	Number of pellets
2¾" (70 mm)	1¼ oz (36 g)	190
3" (76 mm magnum)	1⅜ oz (39 g)	210
3½" (89 mm magnum)	1⁹⁄₁₆ oz (47 g)	235

However, it is not only the weight of the pellet but the speed at which it is travelling that determines whether it can deliver the knock-out blow needed for a clean kill. That brings us on to the question of range. We will consider this in greater detail later, but for the moment the guidance given here is based on the assumption that you will not be shooting at anything beyond 40 yards and that most shots will be taken at 30 yards or less.

The important thing to remember is that there are two basic limiting factors. The pattern of shot spreads out as distance increases; at some point the pattern breaks down and there are insufficient pellets hitting the bird to guarantee a clean kill. The other consideration is the force behind the pellets – called the striking energy – which is a result of the combined weight and speed. This too declines rapidly with distance and reaches a point where the pellet simply doesn't have enough power to penetrate vital organs. Larger shot may kill a goose at 40 yards while small shot may simply injure it.

A comparison of pellet sizes:
(l to r) typical wildfowling sizes, BB, No. 1 and
No. 3 compared with a No. 5, used for game shooting

So the range at which an accurate shot will achieve a clean kill will be limited by whichever of these two factors kicks in first. Surprisingly, the range is not very great and in practice many of the differences would be impossible to judge on the marsh. Using heavier loads or larger shot will not magically increase the range at which you can consistently achieve a clean kill. The variations are surprisingly small. The ultimate limiting factor, therefore, is your skill with the gun.

As with all shooting, the wildfowler should only take a shot which is within the limitations imposed by their own marksmanship and the gun/cartridge combination they are using. It is not acceptable to try a long shot in the hope that you might be lucky, because it won't be lucky for the bird to fly on crippled by a few stray pellets, dying on the marsh days later. And, before stocking up on the heavy artillery, remember again that there is clearly no advantage in using heavy loads when you would shoot more confidently with a standard cartridge.

Remember too that success lies in the right gun/cartridge combination. Just because Old Joe can wallop mallard with an ounce-and-a-quarter of number 3s, don't assume you can do the same. It is very important to pattern your gun to see what pattern it will throw with different loads. Then you can choose the best one for your shooting. For example in a 30" circle you need at least 140 pellets for a small duck (teal), for mallard around 90, and for large geese around 55, based on American research.

Minimum UK shot sizes for wildfowling (in at least 32g loads)

Assuming each cartridge's pattern delivers five or more pellet strikes to the body overall.

Species	Steel*	Bismuth	Tungsten	Hevi-Shot*
Geese	BB	1	1	3
Large duck (mallard)	1	3	4	4
Small duck (teal)	4	5	5	5

* Based on American research.

The table above gives an indication of suitable pellet sizes for different quarry. It will be a useful guideline to start from, but only experience will determine which are really the most effective loads for you, and the most effective materials. At a 30 yard range all the non-lead options, in appropriate loadings, should kill cleanly but they do have different characteristics.

Materials

Bismuth is less dense than lead and more brittle. It also costs at least four times as much. Wildfowlers are less insouciant with their cartridges than game Shots, however, and are likely to use as many cartridges in a season as the game Shot does in a day.

Bismuth is available in a wide range of sizes and weights, and loose shot can be obtained for home loading. It is soft and malleable and can be treated like lead. Because of the difference in density you are generally urged to use at least a size larger than that which would have been recommended for lead (e.g. go to number 1 or BB if you would have used number 3 lead).

Tungsten matrix, although slightly more expensive than bismuth, has gained greater popularity among wildfowlers. It is close to lead in density, but tends to produce variable patterns. It is available in a range of loads, including 12 bore, 10 bore and 8 bore.

Hevi-shot is considerably more expensive than any other options, to lead, Hevi-shot is an alloy of tungsten, nickel and iron. It is denser than lead, and very hard – so hard that the manufacturer recommends that you do not use it unless your gun is designed to shoot steel shot, and even then you should have a minimal degree of choke, nothing more than quarter choke.

Strangely, but helpfully, you do not necessarily have to increase the pellet size because its high density means that it retains more energy than other shot materials – it punches harder. Despite the cost, Hevi-shot has proved popular with wildfowlers and is available for both 12 and 10 bores in a variety of loads.

Steel (soft iron) The least expensive alternative to lead, steel is much harder and significantly less dense. It comes in two forms: standard steel is suitable for standard proof guns and it is always loaded into plastic shot cups to prevent contact with the barrel walls; high performance steel should only be fired through guns that have passed a special steel shot proof, which is signified by the words 'steel shot' and a fleur de lys stamped on the barrels. It will state on the cartridge box whether it contains standard or high performance cartridges.

Although there has been much scepticism and criticism of steel shot, it has been used in the United States and some European countries for many years without any real problems. However it is recommended that you should not use more than half choke, or, with a lightweight game gun, more than a quarter choke to prevent possible bulging of the barrel wall at the choke. It is growing in popularity with UK wildfowlers.

You should use a shot at least two sizes larger than you would with lead and also a heavier load to increase the number of pellets in the shot pattern. There is a very wide range of cartridges available from British and overseas manufacturers for 10 bores, 12 bores and smaller gauges.

A final note of warning: steel shot will rust, so be careful not to get it wet.

Approximate densities of shot in grams per cubic centimetre	
Lead	11.0 g/cc
Bismuth	9.6 g/cc
Tungsten matrix	10.8 g/cc
Steel	7.8 g/cc
Hevi-shot	12.0 g/cc

Patterning

Patterning, or plating, is a way of assessing the pattern of shot which your gun will produce with a particular cartridge. It basically involves shooting at a white-washed plate, or sheet of paper, so that you can see how the pellets are distributed within a central 30" circle.

After firing a number of cartridges you can then see whether you are getting a sufficient concentration of pellets to provide a lethal pattern.

Different sizes of pellets and different load weights will often produce different patterns; plating helps you to determine the most effective cartridge for your gun. BASC has produced a fact sheet which gives full details of patterning; you can find it on the association's website at http://www.basc.org.uk/media/cartridge_patterning_1.pdf

8 TIME AND TIDE WAIT FOR NO MAN

At some time during his reign, which lasted from 1016 to 1035, it is reputed that King Canute went to a beach and commanded the tide to come no further. Allegedly this was to prove to his followers that there were limits even to the royal power. He got wet, but it proved the point. And nothing much has changed over the last thousand years, royalty or not.

If you get caught out on the marsh, the Canute approach is not recommended. The prudent course is to avoid any sticky situations in the first place. The way to do this is to read and understand your tide table. It is the wildfowler's bible. However, before looking at the tide table, it is important to understand the working of the tides themselves.

A tide is the regular and predictable movement of the sea caused by the way the earth, moon and sun move in relation to each other and the gravitational forces these movements create. Because astronomical movements are well known, the tides can be predicted very accurately. These are the figures you will see in your tide table, but they can only be considered as a baseline. There are other influences that introduce much greater uncertainty.

Movements of water caused by the weather, for example wind and atmospheric pressure effects, are called surges. These are not easily predicted. Often the predicted tides and what you actually see happening do not appear to correspond. This is due to surges – either negative or positive – and it is worth remembering that a positive surge can add a great deal of height to a tide.

In most places in the UK there are usually two high tides a day, and these are approximately twelve hours and twenty-five minutes apart. Hence, if high water is at 01:00 hours on Monday morning, it will be at approximately 01:50 hours on Tuesday morning. This can be a handy rough reckoner when planning trips. The cycle of tide heights, however, is not constant, and the height varies during the cycle. When the sun and moon are in line, on opposite sides of the earth, the two reinforce each other's gravitational force and cause higher than average high tides and lower than average low tides. This means that during the period of the new moon and full moon the tide comes in higher and goes out further. These are called 'spring tides'.

When the sun and moon form a right-angle with the earth, lower high tides than average and higher low tides than average are caused. Basically there is less variation between high and low water. These tides are called 'neap tides'. There is also seasonal variation in tide heights, with the highest tides expected around the spring equinox (usually 21 March) and the autumn equinox (usually 23 September).

So, how does all of this relate to the little tide table booklet stuffed in your pocket? The table consists of columns of information, so, on a given

date you can discover what time the two high waters are expected and their predicted heights, at what time the two low waters are expected and their predicted heights, and also the times that the sun and moon rise and set. This is a lot of information to remember with certainty, which is why it is always imperative to carry your table with you when out fowling.

Key points about tide tables

Times in tide tables are listed in GMT (Greenwich Mean Time). Because of this, during British Summer Time in the early part of the wildfowling season you must remember to add one hour to the times listed, until the clocks are put back around the end of October. The table will say this, but it is amazing how easy it is to forget.

The tide heights listed are PREDICTED heights and do not take weather conditions into account.

Tables give the time for a particular port, they then list the adjustments you have to make for other points along the coast. Make sure you check this and then add or subtract the appropriate hours and minutes for the location where you will be shooting.

The tide heights are listed in both metres and feet. Make sure you know the difference between the two, and don't get them confused.

One final important fact about tide tables. They are not waterproof. Keep them in a sealable waterproof bag; then you won't reach into your pocket to double check the time of high water and pull out a lump of illegible mush.

All this information is vital when planning your trip to the marsh, but how do you use it?

In chapter 10 we look in detail at techniques for shooting morning and evening flights, shooting the tide and under the moon. Here we are concerned with the effects of the tide on planning your flight.

Morning flight

Firstly, you will need to know at what time and how big the high tide is expected to be. With a big spring tide you may well get flooded out of your gutter at the front of the marsh.

Your table also tells you what time sunrise is. However, light starts to break about an hour before the sunrise time quoted, so you will need to be in your chosen spot well in advance. This will allow you to be in place when the duck start to move, and will avoid the wrath of other fowlers who were in place in plenty of time. There is little that upsets a fowler more that someone wandering around on the marsh in the middle of a flight. It will usually be explained to you, in no uncertain terms, if you are guilty of this easily avoidable sin.

Tide flight

This is where the high tide is used, as it can cause the birds to move at times other than the normal morning and evening flight times. Again for this type of flighting you need to know the time and height of high water, in order to choose an appropriate spot.

Evening flight

Here you utilise the fading light of evening, which causes the birds to flight to their roosting or feeding grounds, depending on species. Again you need to know if high water is going to have an effect on where or when you shoot, and also what time the sun sets. It is still possible to shoot well after sundown, as it doesn't get dark until around an hour after sunset.

Moon flight

This is perhaps the most exciting form of wildfowling. During the period of the full moon, birds often move using the light of the moon. Here your tide table again tells you what the state of the tide is, but also when moonrise is. Usually it will also tell you a time for the key phases of the moon.

Fowling on the flood

Once the tide starts to make, it can be amazing how quickly it can flood in, particularly on a big spring tide. Make sure you have all your gear together in case you realise you have to get off quickly. Depending on where you are, you may literally only have a couple of minutes to get off, or be faced with sitting the tide out. Even worse is standing the tide out – and don't forget that your dog is a lot shorter than you!

On some marshes it is worth remembering that the tides can sneak around behind you and flood in at the back of the marsh, thus cutting off your exit route. Experienced fowlers in the area are usually more than happy to explain where such areas are and show you the routes on and off the marsh. They will also be able to explain what the weather is doing and how that may affect the tide - which may be dramatic.

sun   **earth**   **moon**

**When the Moon and Sun are in line the
gravitational pull is strongest –
this produces a spring tide.**

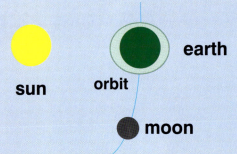

earth

sun   **orbit**

moon

**When the Moon is along the
line of the Earth's orbit around
the Sun, the gravitational pull is at its
weakest – producing a neap tide.**

The moon and tides

The phase of the moon has a double effect on wildfowl. Wild geese in particular alter their flighting times according to the moon's phase. Near the full moon they may well remain on their feeding grounds well into the night and not flight back to their roost until the early hour - an optimistic gunner waiting near the sea wall as the sun sets may not even see a goose. At other times, around the last quarter, geese may flight back to roost at dusk but return to feed in the very early morning as the moon rises. These situations, of course, are more likely to occur when the skies are clear or there is light cloud cover, and the moon provides enough light for the geese to feed by.

To a lesser extent duck will also alter their feeding habits on a moonlit night. The normal pattern of morning and evening flight will be disrupted by moonlight feeding, and many a seasoned wildfowler will claim that there is no experience so magical as shooting geese or wigeon under the moon.

On the coast, the phases of the moon create variations in the range between low and high water. Put simply, when the moon is in its first or last quarter – a half moon – it produces neap tides, and at full moon or new moon we have spring tides. Neap tides have a small tidal range, the difference is visible in that the low tide does not 'go out' very far, and high water often barely reaches the saltings that fringe the exposed mudflats. Spring tides are far more dramatic, with high 'springers' flooding all the marsh right up to the sea wall, and receding way out to expose vast expanses of sand and mudflats.

This constant change in tide levels throughout the lunar calendar has a profound effect on coastal bird life. During the period of neap tides the wildfowl and waders are not flooded off the marsh as there is almost always some land that remains dry and above the high tide mark. Birds are thus prone to move about the estuary or marsh as the tide lifts them, and the wildfowler concealed along the edge of the saltings may have a good tide flight.

During the period of spring tides, the majority of the birds may be forced off the marsh as the tide floods it, and in these situations the shore gunner will plan to intercept them as they flight to some secluded spot inland. Though both of these tactics fall into the tide flighting category, they are very different in location.

Add to this any estimates of how the wind and weather will affect when and where the birds will fly, and you will be able to calculate exactly where to intercept them. Unfortunately wildfowl never read any books on wildfowl behaviour and consistently do their own thing. We, as wildfowlers, may have studied their ways and read the theories at great length, and with all this knowledge we hope to narrow the odds in our favour, but it still comes down to educated guesswork. There are so many factors in the pursuit of these wildest of quarry species over which we have no control, so what every wildfowler hopes for is one other factor – luck.

How the tides flow

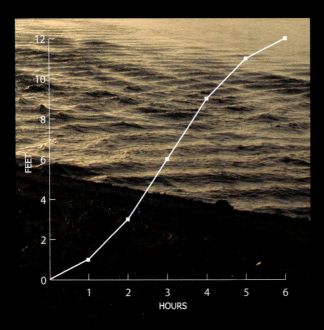

Tides do not ebb and flow at a uniform rate. The tide starts to move slowly, gathers pace and is flowing most strongly at the mid point; then the movement slows down until high or low water is reached.

This movement follows the rule of twelfths.
- 1st hour's rise or fall = $1/12$ of range
- 2nd hour's rise or fall = $2/12$ of range
- 3rd hour's rise or fall = $3/12$ of range
- 4th hour's rise or fall = $3/12$ of range
- 5th hour's rise or fall = $2/12$ of range
- 6th hour's rise or fall = $1/12$ of range

Don't forget...

Take your tide table with you.

Your tide table is in GMT.

Check the weather before you go.

Think about what the weather may do to the tide.

Make sure you know the way off the marsh.

Take your wading staff.

Tell someone where you are going.

Get to know your marsh!

9 ONTO THE MARSH - THE THEORY

The theory of wildfowling is disarmingly simple, as indeed is the equation $e = mc^2$, but all things are relative, and never more so than on the marsh.

The theory states that ducks spend the day roosting out on the shore, at dusk they fly inland to feed – the evening flight – and they return to roost on the shore at dawn – the morning flight. Geese obligingly do the reverse, spending their nights on the shore and their days inland, with the necessary shuttle flights at appropriate times. All the wildfowler needs to do is work out the routes they take from sea to land and back again, sit under the flight path and fill his bag…with ducks, geese and the odd flying pig.

Unfortunately wildfowl are pragmatists, not theoreticians. It may indeed be the middle of the day but if a high tide and a raging gale make life uncomfortable on the marsh many sensible duck will happily look for a sheltered haven inland. That is a fairly obvious example but there are many other more subtle factors, operating alone or in combination, that determine their behaviour. The four predominant influences are the tide, the weather, the moon and the availability of feeding. These will dictate both when and where you should concentrate your efforts.

So how do they operate?

There are plenty of books to give you advice but ultimately they can only provide an informed context within which you can interpret your own experience. Like a taxi driver you need the knowledge, and you won't get that by poring over maps. A map is only the first step – you need a large scale map of the marsh to give you a basic orientation, and on which you can scribble notes, and draw flight lines and conclusions, but never certainties, because the sand is always shifting, channels move, and gutters deepen.

And reconnaissance doesn't have to be boring. The marsh can be a lovely place in summer, so take the dog and go exploring. See it at all stages of the tide, at both spring and neap tides. Walk the channels, study the gutters, work out your routes on and off, remembering that you may need to do this in the pitch dark. A night-time reconnaissance will also prove invaluable in revealing such crucial landmarks as the lights of a farm or factory, which are obviously of far greater value than a clump of bushy-topped trees a mile inland when you are blundering about at midnight. And don't limit your reconnaissance to the shoreline. Look for the inland feeding ground that will attract the birds from the marsh: fields of potatoes and stubble are obvious magnets. It will be a big advantage in predicting flight lines if you know at least one of the birds' likely destinations.

Essential as it is, though, reconnaissance is no substitute for experience and here, if you are lucky, there is a shortcut. Tap into somebody else's experience. Many wildfowling clubs make it a condition of membership that you must spend so much time or so many outings in the company of an experienced member. The intention is that you should be safe, legal and behave in a proper fashion on the marsh, but while you are learning the basics of survival do try to pick up as much as you can of fieldcraft. Make the most of this opportunity and where it is not a rule you would be wise to seek out a member who is prepared to accompany you on a pre-season visit and then take you with them for a few armed sorties. If you are prepared to provide the petrol and maybe a pint or two afterwards you will be well rewarded.

> When you make your reconnaissance there are three key things you are looking for:
>
> • Where the birds roost
> • Where the birds feed
> • The flight lines that they follow at dawn and dusk

Roosting and feeding grounds

A daylight visit with a good pair of binoculars will often show you where some of the wildfowl are roosting but a walk on the marsh will reveal many clues. This should be an essential part of your preparation for a wildfowling foray, but many of us live too far from the marsh or have too little time to organise regular inspections. The answer is simple: arrive early.

Many fowlers decide where they are going on the marsh days before their trip. In fact some only ever go to one or two spots on a marsh, year in year out. They arrive, get kitted up, let the dog out, and they're off. A mad race to the spot they want to be in. Eyes focused on the ground two steps in front, hood up and ears closed. Now this may work, but try arriving a little early and taking a slow walk out to your chosen spot. Look around, and above all listen. It is amazing what you may find out. Maybe the wigeon are feeding on the splashes that you always speed past without a glance. But how do you know? First you have to look. Are there any of the signs illustrated opposite?

All of these signs indicate that the birds are using that area. By examining them, particularly any feathers left lying around from their preening, you can get an idea of which species are frequenting the spot.

Signs to look for

- Footprints around the edges in the soft mud

- Feathers on the water where the birds have been preening

- Little tufts of grass floating on the water from the birds grazing

- Signs of feeding, such as droppings

Flight lines

Most of the time on a marsh there are popular flight lines, such as gutters or creeks, which birds tend to follow. Identifying these, through observation, can be a simple key to success. If you can get yourself under these flight lines, the rest is up to you and your shooting.

There are often key features on a marsh that birds will use as reference points whilst flying between roosting and feeding areas. Large gutters are often the bird equivalent of motorways, with packs of teal or wigeon whizzing past, low and fast. If you find one of these gutters, you can be in for some fast and furious shooting. Points of land that stick out into the water when the tide comes in can also be great spots. The birds often take the shortest route and cut across these points.

Wind

However, these flight lines seldom take the form of narrow corridors where you can happily sit under a steady steam of birds. Flighting duck will use certain routes more than others, but with more experience and,

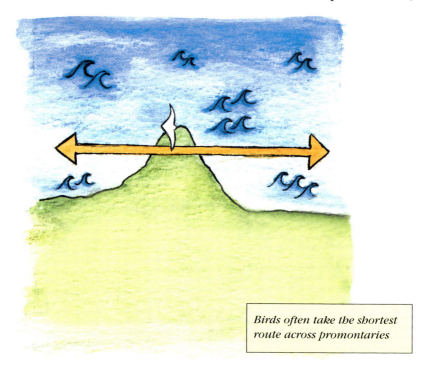

Birds often take the shortest route across promontaries

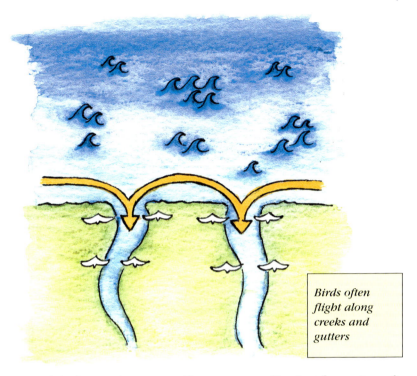

Birds often flight along creeks and gutters

above all, careful observation you will come to realise just how strongly their movements are influenced by weather, and particularly wind strength and direction. There is a lot of truth in the old saying 'the worse the weather the better the fowling'.

In clear weather and light winds flighting wildfowl can easily gain height, so you may see a lot of duck but they will be well beyond shotgun range. In such conditions the birds will be far less inclined to stick to the predicted flight lines and their movements may be over a broad front rather than a narrow flight corridor.

Strong wind gives a much better chance of a shot or two. It is difficult to believe, while you are sitting in a freezing creek looking into an icy north-easter, but wind strength at ground level is considerably less than at even 40 yards above. This is because the moving air is slowed down by friction over ground features. Wildfowl, being sensible creatures, opt to spend less of their energy budget by keeping out of the strong wind and flying low. It is in these conditions that they will more readily follow the channels of any deep creeks or gutters, and this may make it easier for us to intercept them.

This is all very well if the birds are flighting into or across the wind direction. If the general direction of flight takes them downwind they will not use these sheltering features, but will gain height quickly and with the wind beneath their tails come screaming over your head with the speed of an express train. If the birds are within range you will need to use a ridiculous amount of forward lead if you wish to consistently avoid shooting where they have just been.

Wind and tide, a deadly combination

In addition to having a significant effect on the pattern of the flight, strong winds also influence the ebb and flow of tides, a fact that has sent many an unobservant wildfowler prematurely to the great saltmarsh in the sky. Knowledge of the tides is probably the most important information a wildfowler can have – it can mean sport or no sport, life or death. The subject was explained in the previous chapter; do read it again before you plan your trip to the foreshore.

Rain, snow, and fog

Any weather conditions that affect visibility will have a beneficial effect on the fowler's chance of success, but again there are attendant risks that anyone venturing out onto the marsh must know. Of the three types of weather condition listed, rain has the least effect on our wildfowl – the proverbial water off a duck's back – but a rough rain shower or squall may unsettle a few birds and induce them to find a more sheltered site. In these conditions, where visibility is reduced by the rain they will tend to follow landmarks such as the edge of the saltings or the line of a creek, and fly reasonably low in order to maintain knowledge of their whereabouts. The soggy but stoic fowler will be in with a chance, provided their spectacles are not too spattered by raindrops.

There is much anecdotal evidence to suggest that wildfowl can predict changes in the weather far better than our television forecasters. They certainly seem to become very unsettled before the onset of snow, often abandoning their normal morning and evening flights to move about throughout the day. Falling snow reduces visibility down to a very short distance, so any birds that are moving around the marsh need to fly low in order to remain in visual contact with the ground. If the wildfowler is lucky in his or her choice of hide on the marsh, the sport can be very exciting with all manner of duck and even geese suddenly appearing out of the swirling snowflakes from any direction. It is at times like these that your hearing plays an important part in your shooting. Birds flying about the marsh will tend to be more vocal than in clear visibility, so you can anticipate any approaching wildfowl by identifying their calls and getting ready for them to suddenly appear out of the murk.

Fog has the same effect as falling snow. The birds become disorientated and will move about the marsh in a more random fashion than in clearer conditions, and this movement may take place at any time of day. Again they will be flying low in order to find recognisable landmarks and therein lies the fowler's opportunity. However, if rain, snow and fog serve to disorientate the wildfowl that live on the marsh, they also dramatically reduce the fowler's chance of getting off the marsh alive.

On some estuaries dense fog can envelop the marsh in a matter of minutes, and all landmarks and other points of reference are quickly lost to sight. Suddenly there is a huge surge in the importance of that magnetic compass you stowed in the recesses of your wildfowling rucksack - it may save your life. Sound becomes muted in fog or falling snow, so the distant rush of the surf at the tide's edge seems to come from all directions and you can't get a fix on it. It may be fanciful, but in fog a rising tide seems to become more sinister - quietly and quickly filling the creeks and gullies and cutting off your escape route to dry land.

There is an additional safety factor that anyone out shooting in a snowstorm must consider. As a wildfowler, you always take great care not to dip the end of your gun into the mud, so it is natural that you hold the gun with the barrels pointing skyward. But in a snowstorm there is the added risk of some large snowflakes entering the muzzles of the gun and creating a partial blockage - check your barrels frequently and be sure to remove any snowflakes before even considering loading the chamber.

10 ONTO THE MARSH ~ THE FIRST SORTIE

Once you have done the basic reconnaissance, and are thoroughly familiar with your tide table, it's time to plan the armed foray. Just as the tide governs your approach to the shore it also determines the behaviour of wildfowl. But they face added complications. They can't pack their lunch into a sandwich box to carry with them - and there's usually something hanging about waiting to kill them.

Feeding and roosting are the keys to their movements. During the season many species will feed inland, where fields of potatoes, stubble or lakes within easy flying distance of the shore will attract them. Making a note of these will give you an idea where the birds are heading for when they leave the shore – or where they will be flying from as they flight out to their roosts. Put the factors together and a pattern emerges; there are four basic times when wildfowl are on the move and you can shoot them:

- Morning flight
- Evening flight
- On the tide
- Under the moon.

Obviously some of these can overlap, and where a rising tide coincides with the evening flight your chancces may be improved. But all of these are governed by the weather. On a stormy day there may be no flight at all. The ducks will simply spend all their time on sheltered creeks or flashes. If the tide is ebbing and the storm is blowing onshore you can walk-up the marsh and expect some good sport. But these are exceptional days; on most outings you will be shooting the flight or the tide.

Drake teal

MORNING FLIGHT

Morning flight is the stuff of romance – but it seldom seems like that as you drag yourself from a warm bed into the freezing winter night. It really does make sense to have everything laid out and checked the night before. And leave yourself ample time – it is a cardinal sin to go blundering onto the marsh just as the sun is rising. You need to be in place on the marsh at least an hour before sunrise. Arriving later may spoil your chances of sport and, worse still, ruin it for any other wildfowler.

This means you should have a very clear idea of where you are going and the route to get there in the dark. Using a torch will disturb birds but most people's night vision is, surprisingly, quite adequate.

At first light ducks that have been feeding inland will head out to sea to rest for the day. Although they may roost on a sandbank to preen and doze they are more vulnerable there and tend to prefer bobbing about on the water. That's fine on a fine day, but not much fun if you're being bounced and buffeted by steep waves and a gale. In these conditions ducks will seek out sheltered bays or creeks that offer some protection.

Now, it follows that when heading for an offshore destination on a clear morning the duck will be flying high – almost invariably out of range of the shore gunner. This is why foul weather is the fowler's friend. Heading into a gale, and looking for shelter, the ducks should be relatively low and slow – they will be within range, at least vertically.

Unfortunately, even in perfect hurricane conditions you cannot be sure of a flight. Duck can be unpredictable and occasionally the flight just fails to happen. It can also vary for no very obvious reason. Duck are quite happy to fly in the dimmest half light, so do be prepared as soon as it's bright enough to see. And don't give up too soon. In general you can expect the flight to be over about an hour after sunrise. But, as always, the weather has the last say and foul weather can substantially delay the flight.

In contrast to the ducks, geese will be flighting from the coast to inland feeding grounds at dawn, but the same rules of weather apply – the worse the better. They tend to flight later than the duck, and this can present you with a quandary. If there are geese out on the sandbanks they will very likely be disturbed if you shoot at duck. You may decide that you would rather have a certain shot at mallard than a possible shot at greylags. But what if there are other fowlers on the marsh aiming for a goose? The rules of good sportsmanship apply.

EVENING FLIGHT

This is the morning flight in reverse, and for the novice wildfowler it is generally the preferred option. Apart from the fact that you are wide awake and have had all day to prepare, it has the advantage that you are going out onto the marsh in daylight. You can indulge in a bit of reconnaissance. This allows you to pick your spot with more discrimination, having looked out for signs of wildfowl, and maybe to find a more convenient hole to hide in – or even to create your own hole.

It also means that you can mark your way off the marsh, if you need to, either by lights on the shore or markers on the saltings. The sands pilot on Morecambe Bay always plotted the old coaching route with branches of laurel, but you can probably find driftwood, or make your own little markers. You can also use a torch, if you need it, and if it will not disturb other fowlers.

Flight times can be extremely unpredictable in the evening. In rough weather duck may start to move while it is full daylight. On a fine night it may be almost too dark to shoot before the birds start to move. Again the weather will determine whether the birds are likely to be flying within range. If they are not, at least the pub will be open.

SHOOTING THE TIDE

When waterfowl are resting or feeding on the shore a rising tide will push them off. Some birds may be happy enough to take to the water and ride out the tide. Some may simply make for higher sandbanks or marsh that is not submerged. Or they may feed at the edge of the tide, coming in with it. And some will simply head off inland to somewhere more convenient.

As always various other factors will decide which option the birds take; the height of the tide, whether it is day or night, calm or rough weather, and the phase of the moon may all play a part. However, if there is a good tide it is a fairly certain bet that wildfowl will be on the move somewhere, so the wildfowler is in with a chance. He or she is also increasing the chance of being drowned. If you shoot the tide it is imperative to know the exact times and height, to be able to adjust the predictions according to the weather and to know which parts of the marsh will remain above water.

Listen to the shipping forecasts. If you are shooting anywhere on the east coast of Britain, beware of strong north-westerly winds in sea area Fair Isle. This will have the effect of pushing more water into the North Sea and the tide may be considerably higher than the table predicts. For Wales and the west coast estuaries, a strong south-westerly in sea area Fastnet piles water up the Bristol Channel and into the Irish Sea, with the same consequences for high tides as far north as the Solway.

If you have this knowledge, and only if you have it, there are two principal ways of shooting the tide.

If you can find cover, or can camouflage yourself on a part of the marsh that will not be submerged, you can sit out the tide, hopefully getting some shooting as the tide flows in around you and then again as it ebbs. This can be a magical experience but – there's always a but – think about quarry retrieval. You will probably need a dog to recover any birds you shoot, and more than one brave retriever has been lost in a strong tide. Keep away from main channels and never shoot if the tide is pulling too strongly.

You can also shoot by backing inland with the advancing tide. This is normally done at night when you are less visible, though there must be sufficient moonlight and light cloud to make the birds stand out in silhouette against the sky. In some places it is possible to crouch at the edge of the tide, retreating as it makes towards the shore. Here you may get a shot at any duck that are flighting along the tideline, provided you remain absolutely still as they approach and don't swivel your face in their direction, shining like a great full moon. To be effective this demands a good knowledge of the shoreline and the tides - and chest waders.

SHOOTING UNDER THE MOON

On a calm night with a bright moon many ducks and geese will be actively feeding and moving on the marsh. However, it is only possible to shoot if you can see them as silhouettes against the sky, and for that you need light cloud cover. Either of the two methods for shooting the tide can be used. Remember that at night camouflage is little use, though anything that is likely to reflect the moonlight should be avoided – and that means covering your face and hands. The important thing is not to move. Standing or crouching you might be another stump or heap of flotsam. Wagging your head or moving your arms will give the game away.

Night shooting of wildfowl can be the most exciting of experiences, but it can also be the most frustrating. Ideal moon flighting conditions only happen, if you'll pardon the expression, once in a blue moon. For the shooter to see the duck in the hours of darkness requires a particular combination of conditions.

First, and most obviously, the moon must be bright enough to provide sufficient light – this is usually three, or at most four, days either side of the full moon.

Next there is the quality of cloud cover. The full moon may be blazing down and birds may be flighting all round you, but on a clear starry night you will have no chance of seeing them. Billowing clouds back-lit by the moon, as described in the poem *The Highwayman* – when "the moon was a ghostly galleon tossed upon cloudy seas" – will improve your chances of catching fleeting glimpses of your quarry. However, the best conditions are when a thin veil of cloud lights up the whole sky, and these conditions may only happen once or twice each season. Misty or hazy conditions may also produce enough back-lit sky to allow the fowler a chance of seeing birds, particularly when a rising full moon is still quite low above the horizon.

There is the added complication that the individual's ability to see in near darkness – their night sight – can vary tremendously. A person with good night vision may be able to use the feeble light of a half moon to good effect while someone who is virtually night blind may not even see birds under ideal cloud conditions strongly lit by a full moon.

One or two points must be remembered when shooting under the moon. As already stated, concealment is not as important as when dawn, dusk, or tide flighting, but sitting or standing still is, and that includes your dog.

Though a well-lit night sky may give clearer viewing than the half-light of dusk or dawn, birds will still only appear as silhouettes against a lighter backdrop, and usually they will be visible only as an indistinct and fast-moving blur. Therefore your ability to identify your quarry by calls, wingbeats, and flight is vitally important. You must be absolutely certain that the fleeting blur you see under the moon is a legitimate target before even thinking of pulling the trigger – if in doubt, don't!

Finally, bear in mind that duck are nocturnal feeders and it makes little difference to them if the marsh is bathed by moonlight, so there is a possibility that they will move about from one feeding ground to another throughout the night, and you may be lucky enough to intercept them at any hour. Geese, on the other hand, are daylight feeders, and they will only move around at night if there is enough light for them to navigate and feed by. After full moon, when the moon rises later in the night, they will usually flight back from their inland feeding grounds to their roosts at dusk, but will then flight back to their feeding areas after moonrise, much to the consternation of the fowler out for a dawn flight.

Moon flighting is an exciting sport, but for every one occasion when all the conditions come right, there will be many more when you suffer the frustration of having wildfowl flighting all round you without catching even the briefest glimpse of one.

Your ability to identify your quarry by calls, wingbeats and flight is vitally important.

11 PULLING THE BIRDS

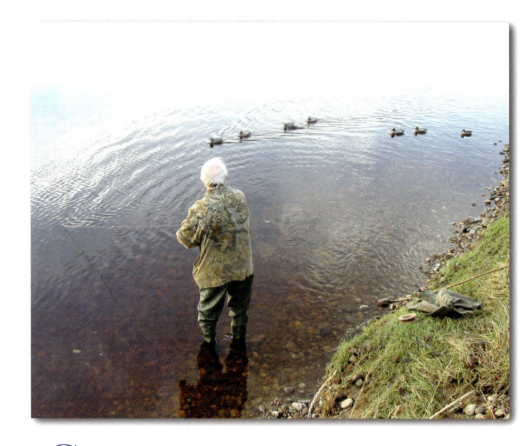

Sometimes the geography of the marsh prevents you from getting directly under a flight line, and even if you can achieve that, flight lines are often a very broad track. To get your quarry within 30 yards may need something more than fieldcraft: this is where decoys and calls come in.

Decoys are used to bring quarry within a range where the fowler is confident of achieving a clean kill. But, as you may expect, it's not just a case of throwing a few plastic ducks onto the water and expecting the birds to pile in. Let's look at duck decoys. They come in a bewildering variety of shapes, sizes and species, so where do you start?

Firstly you need to think about the type of shooting you will be doing. If your shooting only involves a short walk from the car you could consider the magnums, which are now readily available. If, however, you have a two-mile slog across sticky mud and deep creeks to get to your spot, you may well want to consider something less bulky.

There is a huge variety of calls to imitate every species of waterfowl...

...and there are decoys for every species too

Alongside size, we also have to consider pattern. Choice of species is always a bone of contention among fowlers: do you need to have the same species in your pattern as you hope to shoot? Most fowlers agree that it is the duck shape on the water that is most important, and not the actual colours of the decoys. One trip out onto a muddy

Plastic teal (above) and shoveler

marsh and your decoys are a matt brown anyway. In a large pattern you may often have a mixture of different species including mallard, wigeon, teal, tufted, pintail and even shoveler, and it usually seems to work. However, if you have the prospect of a long walk on the foreshore, you may find it more convenient to use teal decoys exclusively. They are small and therefore you can get an effective number in your bag without taking up all the space or the bag being too heavy to carry.

The keel question

Apart from size and species the actual design of the decoys is something you need to consider. This brings us to the keel question

Weighted, suction or Aquakeel? Aqua what? Some decoys come with a keel that fills with water, and that is what gives them their stability and keeps them upright. They are fantastic

if you can place your decoys on the water, and they hugely reduce the weight for carrying. However, there are a couple of practical problems when using Aquakeel decoys. The first is that if you have to throw your decoys out to get them onto the water, they have an infuriating tendency to land upside down. You may manage to avoid this problem by inserting a weight inside the keel, which only slightly increases the weight, but does get them landing the right way up. Also, when you get your decoys in at the end of the flight, it is a physical impossibility to get all of the water out of the keel, so you can end up with a very wet bag.

You can also buy suction keel decoys. These have a concave base that sucks down onto the water. They can work well, especially if the tide goes out, as they then sit flat on the mud, rather than at an angle as keeled ones do. But they still land upside down if you throw them out.

Weighted keel decoys land the right way up, but of course they increase the weight you have to carry, though some of the more modern designs are lighter. Most fowlers end up with a mixture from which they choose those that seem most appropriate for the particular day's shooting.

A strip weight

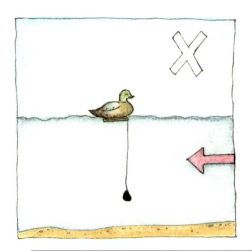 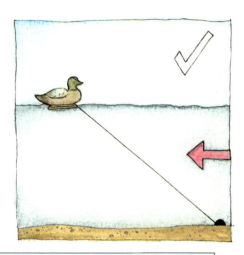

The mooring line should be three times the depth of the water

Weights and lines

Mooring your decoys is important – and not just from the financial point of view. They must not only be secure but also appear in a formation that will attract flighting duck. The key factors are accessibility, the pull of the tide and the firmness of the bottom. In practice this means using either a peg or a weight on the end of your line. If you can't get out to put the pegs in the ground they have to be weighted down.

If the tide pull is light where you shoot you may well get away with fishing weights. A very popular design of weights is the 'strap lead'. It is exactly that – a strap of lead that anchors the decoy but at the end of the flight is then wrapped round the neck to keep everything tidy. These are excellent, provided the tide isn't too strong. Where there is a fierce current you will find the kind of lead weights used by sea fishermen are most effective.

The choice of line you can use is again almost endless. Many people use heavy breaking strain fishing line – this is great as it doesn't absorb water, but it has a tendency to tangle. Much better, if you can find one, is an old fly line. Para cord is also good, but it soaks up water, and is liable to rot. There is a custom-made product called 'no tangle line', which is made from PVC and doesn't soak up water, cut your fingers or rot; it is widely available in the USA but may be difficult to find in the UK.

A gang rig

Single or gang?

All fowlers have their own special way of rigging their decoys, usually developed over many years of trial and error, but they usually follow one of two basic ideas.

The single-line system is a weight and line for each decoy. This is great for splashes, ponds and areas without too much tidal pull. The key thing is the length of the line. If it is too short the decoy will be pulled under, or lift the weight and float away downstream (see page 83). A good rule of thumb is for the line to be three times the depth of the water. It pays, therefore, to have several yards of line attached and only let out as much as is necessary.

A gang rig uses a single weight for all the decoys, with each one attached to the line coming from that weight. This allows you to use only the one heavy weight for up to about half a dozen decoys.

Pattern

Most fowlers agree that positioning is more important than pattern. You need to put the decoys somewhere where duck are likely to be. You also need to think about the direction of approaching birds, as that has an effect on the positioning of your decoys. It usually works well if you put your decoys slightly upwind of your position, as approaching birds will usually try to land into the wind.

But the key thing about placing decoys is range. The whole idea of decoys is to bring the birds within the range at which you can consistently kill. In general decoys should be between 20 and 30 yards away, so that birds approaching the back of the pattern are still in range. This is even more important with steel shot, as it loses velocity at a shorter range than other shot types.

Setting out the decoys

The call of the wild

There are few sounds more evocative than the cry of wildfowl across the marsh – and few things more satisfying for the wildfowler than being able to imitate them. There is a huge thrill when your call is answered by wild birds and they wheel away from their intended course, drawn by the sound.

There are basically three kinds of calls: those that are blown, those which are squeezed and the human voice box. Recordings and electronic calls are illegal. The commonest calls are those, made of wood or plastic, which you blow, usually cupping your hands to alter the pitch and quality of the sound. They are often made for a particular species and it helps to become familiar with the call so that you can imitate it. Some websites contain bird calls and there are various bird guides on DVD that include the calls.

There are also calls which provide their own wind – from a sort of built-in concertina. Finally, there is that wonderful instrument, the human voice – easily portable, infinitely adaptable, hard to mislay and ready on the instant. It has to be admitted that geese in particular will occasionally respond to the most inept efforts, but there are some wildfowlers who have developed their calling into an art.

Calls are available for virtually every species of duck and goose

Many wildfowlers use camouflage netting to build a hide on the marsh…

…but most use whatever natural cover is available. However, you should check that building hides or digging-in is permitted on your marsh.

12 WILDFOWLING DOGS

The vagaries of nature mean that few things can be said about wildfowling with absolute certainty. But there is one inescapable fact – you need a reliable dog on hand whenever you go.

The choice of breed is always a subjective judgement and most owners will admit a degree of sentiment, which is not entirely out of place – always choose a dog you feel comfortable with. But there are some objective criteria to apply in selecting a wildfowling dog. It is sensible to consider why you need a dog, what you expect it to do and how it will fit with any other shooting interests.

The fowler's dog should be fit, active – and love water

Because wildfowling takes place over water, or close to it, shot birds must often be retrieved quickly before they are swept away by currents, tides or the wind. Bearing in mind that the very best wildfowling takes place in stormy weather – often in the depths of winter – the requirements for the fowler's dog begin to take shape. Add to that equation the species of birds that may have to be retrieved – from a diminutive teal to a large and heavy goose – and we begin to form a picture of a dog that must be both hardy and strong. As the fowler may spend long hours crouching in a hide waiting for the chance of a shot, his dog also needs to be gentle and patient.

A number of breeds may fulfil these criteria; the novice, however, is probably wisest to opt for a labrador or a springer spaniel. These breeds have a proven record of ability and trainability. Both will perform adequately on the shore and each is suited to other branches of shooting sport.

By reputation labradors are slightly easier to train than spaniels. Maybe the difference is not quite as distinct as imagined by the commentator who observed that 'most labradors are born half-trained; most spaniels die half-trained', but there is a general acceptance that the former is a particularly suitable choice for a first attempt at gundog training. What is crucially important, with either breed, is that a puppy is obtained from proven working parentage. At all costs avoid show strains, which can suffer from generations of selective breeding concentrated upon visual appearance rather than working abilities.

In general it is best to avoid the HPR (hunt, point, retrieve) breeds such as the German shorthaired pointer, vizsla or Weimaraner because it is doubtful whether their very short coats give adequate protection in bitterly cold and wet conditions. Many a wildfowler has watched his black labrador turn white as ice crystals formed on its coat within minutes of retrieving a goose from among the ice-floes on a winter estuary. A retriever or spaniel will happily cope with such conditions, but less well-insulated breeds might suffer from repeated immersions in icy brine.

In 2006 BASC published the results of a gundog survey. This showed that, amongst those members who owned gundogs, labradors were the most popular breed, closely followed by springer spaniels. Other breeds, such as golden and flatcoated retrievers, also have their devotees and, especially in the eyes of coastal fowlers, there is a growing interest in American breeds such as the Chesapeake Bay retriever and the Nova Scotia duck tolling retriever.

Training your puppy will follow the normal course for any gundog and there are plenty of books and videos on the market. If you lack the time or confidence you can go to a professional or buy a dog that is already trained.

One aspect of training that is particularly important for the wildfowler is being able to handle your dog reliably at a distance. There are two reasons why remote handling is vital on the foreshore. Firstly, because the fowler may be concealed in dense reed beds or crouching in a muddy

The Chesapeake Bay retriever is becoming increasingly popular with wildfowlers

gutter, his dog may not be in a position to accurately mark the fall of a shot duck or goose. In these circumstances it is helpful to be able to direct the dog to the approximate location of the fall by whistle and hand signals.

The second reason is even more important. It is in the nature of wildfowling that occasionally your dog might be placed in a potentially dangerous situation. For example, if a bird is being swept away by a particularly strong current, or planes down to drop a long way out on a very stormy sea, it may be absolutely essential to recall your dog before he or she gets into trouble. In these circumstances a whistle carries much better than the human voice, so ensure that the whistle 'stop' and 'recall' commands are reliably obeyed before taking your young dog out on a windswept estuary.

Taking care with the basics always pays dividends and, if you have observed the elementary rules, by the time a pup is about eighteen months old, it should be well on the way to becoming a real asset at flight time. Apart from earning its keep by retrieving shot wildfowl, a good gundog will be a fine companion on the marsh and a joy to work.

Labrador

When, in the nineteenth century, the Earl of Malmesbury and the Duke of Buccleuch created the modern labrador retriever for use on their grouse moors and partridge manors, they could have had little idea that their 'genetic engineering' would eventually result in a breed that is superbly suited to modern wildfowling. Developed from the lesser Newfoundland dog, bred by fishermen working the cruel seas of eastern Canada, its short double coat provides excellent insulation and is ideal for working in water. The lab is a strong swimmer and powerful enough to retrieve a goose in a strong current. Their placid temperament is well suited to spending hours quietly sitting by the Gun's side, whether it is on the marsh, in a pigeon hide or on the peg at a driven shoot. They are also excellent family dogs.

Labrador retriever – the fowler's favourite

Springer spaniel

While the springer is not purpose-built for wildfowling it remains a popular choice. The long coat can be a disadvantage, particularly in ice and snow, and springers rarely enjoy long periods of inactivity. However, many fowlers walk the marsh for snipe, rabbits, or the odd stray pheasant and here the springer's ability to hunt and flush is an enormous benefit.

Certainly, if the major component of the sportsman's year is to involve rough shooting or walked-up game, then a springer may be the best choice as it will busily flush game from the densest of cover. A spaniel is also a superb breed for taking onto the beating line in formal shoots.

The springer is a fine all-rounder

Look after your dog

Wildfowling places great demands on a dog, and its welfare should always be your primary concern. A neoprene camouflaged coat provides warmth, buoyancy and concealment, and if a dog is going to be sitting in wet mud for hours something to sit on is a good idea.

Finally always rub down and dry your dog before putting it back in your vehicle; make sure it is warm and remember it probably appreciates a good meal.

13 WILDFOWLING AND CONSERVATION

One of 11 marshland sites in Essex secured for shooting with the help of the WHT

Shooting and conservation are two sides of the same coin. Shooting can only continue when it is sustainable, and that means wildlife must be managed to ensure there is a surplus that can be shot. Shoot too much and soon there will be nothing left to shoot.

But in most areas shooting is regulated by clubs who monitor shooting through bag returns to help ensure that the pressure from shooting presents no threat.

Wildfowling clubs manage more than 105,000 hectares of coastal land, 90 per cent of which is in Sites of Special Scientific Interest. They also manage areas within national and local nature reserves as well as maintaining their own reserves.

Many clubs are actively involved in conservation work, improving habitat for wildfowl on the land they control. These may be ambitious schemes bringing cattle onto the marsh to create the kind of habitat needed by ground-nesting waders, or very simple initiatives like clearing litter and rubbish from the shoreline.

Wildlife Habitat Trust

One way in which the shooting community shows its commitment to conservation is through the Wildlife Habitat Trust. This fund, maintained by voluntary contributions, helps clubs to buy land so that it can be managed for the benefit of shooting and wildlife.

Since it was founded by BASC in 1986, the trust has enabled shooters to buy more than 3,000 acres of land, valued at more than £1.5 million, and has given more than £84,000 in grants for conservation projects.

The money is advanced by the trustees, either as a grant or loan, to projects throughout the UK and in some cases to overseas initiatives which have an impact on the migratory wildfowl which winter in the UK.

The trust, which was founded by BASC, raises funds by selling an annual duck stamp, badge and other collectables. Many of the UK's finest wildlife artists have produced images for the WHT and the new stamp is launched annually at the CLA Game Fair.

To find out more about the Wildlife Habitat Trust you can visit its website www.wht.org.uk or telephone 01244 573014.

WILDFOWLING PERMITS AND CONTACTS

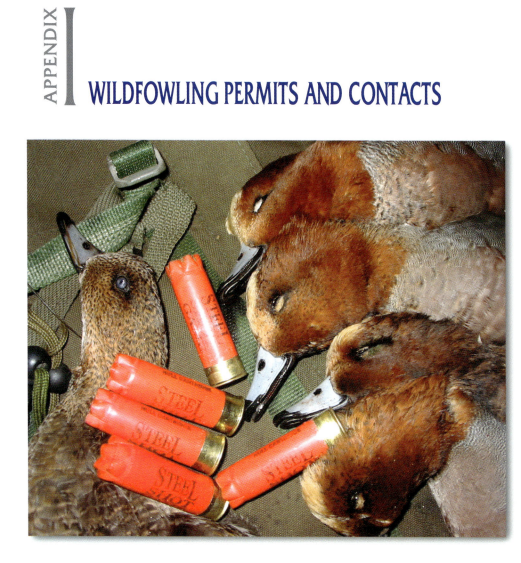

BASC members have access to an exclusive scheme that provides opportunities to shoot wildfowl all around the coast of the UK.

The wildfowling permit scheme involves 38 BASC affiliated clubs, from Cornwall to Cromarty who will issue day tickets to members. A free guide to the scheme, which also includes valuable information on fieldcraft, safety and the law, is available from the conservation and land management department at Marford Mill.

In most cases, unless you are very experienced, a member of the club will accompany you on the foreshore. This can provide an excellent introduction to the sport and a chance to experience it without making an immediate commitment.

You will find details of many wildfowling clubs that have vacancies for members on the BASC-managed website www.goshooting.com. Some of the more popular clubs may have a waiting list so if you cannot find a club in the area where you hope to shoot contact the BASC membership services department on 01244 573021 and they will try to help you.

The cost of club membership varies considerably and usually reflects the amount of shooting available. Some of the larger clubs also have inland areas and game shoots.

Contacts

BASC Head Office
British Association for
Shooting & Conservation,
Marford Mill, Rossett, Wrexham
LL12 OHL
Tel: 01244 573000
e-mail: enq@basc.org.uk

BASC Scotland
BASC Scottish Centre,
Trochry, Dunkeld,
Tayside,
PH8 0DY
Tel: 01350 723 226
email: scotland@basc.org.uk

BASC Northern Ireland
BASC Northern Ireland Centre,
33 Castle Street,
Lisburn, Co Down,
BT27 4SP
Tel: 028 9260 5050
email: nire@basc.org.uk

BASC Wales
BASC Wales Centre,
The Station House,
Caersws, Powys,
SY17 5HH
Tel: 01686 688 861
email: wales@basc.org.uk

website: www.basc.org.uk

II WILDFOWLING QUARRY SPECIES AND THE LAW

W ildfowling is governed by the Wildlife and Countryside Act (1981) and the Wildlife Order (Northern Ireland) (1985).

The species of birds that can be legally killed or taken by permitted means outside the close seasons are listed below.

DUCKS	GEESE	WADERS	OTHERS
Gadwall	Canada goose	Common snipe	Coot[2]
Goldeneye	Greylag goose	Curlew[1]	Moorhen[2]
Mallard	Pink-footed goose	Golden plover	
Pintail	White-fronted goose[3]	Jack snipe[1]	
Pochard		Woodcock	
Scaup[1]			
Shoveler			
Teal		Notes: Northern Ireland only[1] England, Wales and	
Tufted duck		Scotland only[2] England and Wales only[3]	
Wigeon			

Open/shooting seasons for wildfowl (ducks and geese) and other species according to the above Acts are shown in the table below. (All dates are inclusive.)

Wildfowl in Northern Ireland anywhere	1 September – 31 January
Wildfowl in England, Wales and Scotland in or over any area below the mean high water mark of ordinary spring tides	1 September – 20 February
Wildfowl in England, Wales and Scotland above the mark	1 September – 31 January
Coot (England, Wales and Scotland only)	1 September – 31 January
Moorhen (England, Wales and Scotland only)	1 September – 31 January
Common snipe	12 August – 31 January
Jack snipe (Northern Ireland only)	1 September – 31 January
Curlew (Northern Ireland only)	1 September – 31 January
Woodcock (England, Wales and NI)	1 October – 31 January
Woodcock (Scotland)	1 September – 31 January
Golden plover	1 September – 31 January

Canada geese

Canada geese have now been added to the open general licences in England – commonly referred to as the pest list.

This means that they can be shot outside the main shooting season for the purposes stated on the general licence:

- for the purpose of preventing the spread of disease
- for preventing serious damage to livestock, foodstuffs for livestock, crops, vegetables, fruit, growing timber, fisheries or inland waters
- for the purpose of preserving public health and safety.

It will not be necessary for individuals to hold copies of the general licences, though you are recommended to make yourself familiar with them. They can be found on the BASC and Defra websites. Anyone shooting listed pest species under general licence must fully comply with the relevant terms and conditions.

According to the conditions sporting shooting alone is not a reason for control. If challenged, the individual would have to show that any shooting of Canada geese, outside the open season, was carried out in accordance with the terms of the appropriate general licence.

This means that in England Canada geese can be shot as a sporting quarry during the wildfowling season, and outside that season they can be controlled as a pest in accordance with the general licences.

Shooting on Sunday and at night

England and Wales. Before the passing of the Wildlife and Countryside Act (1981), orders prohibiting the shooting of wildfowl on Sundays were made under the Protection of Birds Act (1954). These orders have not been rescinded, and so the following counties/part counties are still affected: Anglesey, Brecknock, Caernarfon, Cardigan, Carmarthen, Cornwall, Denbigh, Devon, Doncaster, Glamorgan, Great Yarmouth County Borough, Isle of Ely, Leeds County Borough, Merioneth, Norfolk, Pembroke, Somerset, North and West Ridings of Yorkshire.

Scotland. Wildfowl and waders may not be shot on Sundays or Christmas Day.

England, Scotland and Wales. Wildfowl may be shot at night.

Northern Ireland. All wild birds protected on Sundays, Christmas Day and at night.

APPENDIX III
WATERFOWL SHOOTING AND SEVERE WEATHER

In periods of severe winter weather (usually when freezing weather conditions are persistent) the relevant government ministers have the power to make a protection order suspending the shooting of wildfowl and waders.

When is a ban enforced?

The shooting of wildfowl and waders is normally suspended after fifteen consecutive days of severe weather – or thirteen days in Northern Ireland.

If after eight days the severe weather looks set to continue BASC contacts all its clubs and syndicates, calling for voluntary restraint where appropriate and warning that a shooting ban is likely. If the hard weather continues for a further five days and looks likely to continue the minister may sign a protection order banning all wildfowl and wader shooting from the fifteenth day.

Throughout this period, information on local weather conditions and waterfowl numbers and behaviour is closely monitored all around the country through BASC regional offices. Voluntary restraint is left to the wildfowling clubs and individual wildfowler's discretion because conditions may vary around the country but guidelines are available from BASC and you are expected to act responsibly.

The final decision on a ban is made jointly by the Department of Environment Food and Rural Affairs, Joint Nature Conservation Committee, Royal Society for the Protection of Birds, Wildfowl and Wetlands Trust and BASC. All of these bodies are consulted, particularly BASC, before a protection order is signed. The order will be widely publicised in the national and local media.

How long does a ban last?

A ban normally lasts for fourteen days; it is reviewed after seven and could be lifted early if a thaw sets in, unless it is considered necessary to give birds more time to regain condition after the freeze. If the weather looks likely to continue a second order may be signed, imposing the ban for a further fourteen days.

The ban may cover the whole of Great Britain, just Scotland, or just England and Wales. Northern Ireland has its own, similar, arrangements. If you are in any doubt, contact your country or regional BASC office.

When the ban is lifted there will be a publicity campaign by BASC and the relevant government departments through announcements in the national and sporting press and, where possible, on television and radio. If you are in any doubt, you should contact your BASC regional office where a 24-hour telephone information service will be available.

Which species are affected?

When a protection order is signed, it becomes an offence to kill or take any of the following species, whether on the coast or inland:

Ducks:	Mallard, teal, wigeon, pintail, tufted duck, pochard, shoveler, gadwall, goldeneye, scaup (Northern Ireland)
Geese:	Greylag, pink-footed, white-fronted, Canada
Waders:	Golden plover, woodcock, common snipe, jack snipe and curlew (Northern Ireland)
Others:	Moorhen, coot

Game birds are not affected, except woodcock, but reared duck are included

NB: Shooting of geese for crop protection during any statutory suspension period is also prohibited unless it is otherwise permitted by licence. Any such shooting should be conducted to minimise unnecessary disturbance to other waterfowl.

It is in the shooting community's interest to be seen to respond responsibly during prolonged severe weather, even though wildfowl and waders may not always show signs of suffering from the conditions. We have gained much respect by our actions in the past, and must not jeopardise this by thoughtless or irresponsible behaviour.

INDEX